PROGRAMMED INSTRUCTION IN ONLINE LEARNING

PROGRAMMED INSTRUCTION IN ONLINE LEARNING

Reinaldo L. Canton

CAMBRIA PRESS

YOUNGSTOWN, NEW YORK

Library of Congress Cataloging-in-Publication Data

Canton, Reinaldo L.
    Programmed instruction in online learning / Reinaldo L. Canton.
        p. cm.
    Includes bibliographical references and index.
    ISBN 978-1-934043-36-3 (alk. paper)
    1. Computer-assisted instruction. 2. Instructional systems--Design. I. Title.

    LB1028.5.C354 2007
    371.33′4--dc22

2007010026

For my Family

TABLE OF CONTENTS

LIST OF FIGURES

LIST OF TABLES

FOREWORD

Most of education is still largely passive. Instructors talk and learners listen. We know that a driver learns more about a route than an accompanying passenger; yet today, learners too often remain "passengers" in our schools, training programs, and even in much of web-based instruction. Research reported herein verified the importance of learner participation. The programmed instruction (PI) format guaranteed *meaningful* student interaction via computer-based demands.

When one teaches swimming, one would expect to produce good swimmers. When teaching graphing, learners should then graph data well. This research verified performance by analyzing performance outcomes, not learner opinions, something not often done in research. It did not take the easy way out by using questionnaires for its primary data. It did not find educationally important differences between the treatments using this performance method, but the research proceeded in the right direction to pursue them.

Instruction in both treatment conditions conformed to the theoretical philosophy that instruction is most efficient when it is cumulative, linear, and densely reiterative. Yes, exploratory learning is important, but not when the instructor has clear terminal performance objectives. In this study, software required learner performance evaluation at the rate of 1–3 times per minute—in the programmed instruction format. That format required 359 learner "thinking" responses during the tutorials. Participation in the PI treatment condition was *overt construction*—not selection / recognition. This is a far more difficult task for students and significant because of this. It is also a more difficult task for computer software programming—especially via the web.

An important contribution of this study was the combination of measurement technologies drawn from *applied behavior analysis* (for the graphing performance task), computer technology, and a knowledge base arising from operant learning research. Its great strength is the blending of divergent fields.

"Treatment integrity" refers to the issue of whether an instructional technique is delivered precisely, consistently, and in the way described. A significant contribution of this study was to expose the lack of control that exists when instruction is accomplished at a distance and not under the close scrutiny of the creator of the instruction. We all avoid work—the things we have to do. Much of learning is not for the "fun of it" and students often take shortcuts.

In summary, this research revealed that some students escaped or avoided contingencies that might have been beneficial to them. The experimental results might have been quite different if 40 percent of students couldn't have supplemented their learning through their own devices. For this, and the other reasons I have mentioned, I believe this research is truly trailblazing. It should prove helpful in the design of future research and application in the field of online instruction.

Professor Darrel E. Bostow
College of Education
University of South Florida

PREFACE

Completed in May 2003, the goal of this study was to determine if a difference in performance occurred among students presented with lesson plans using active, programmed instruction using constructed-response contingencies, and passive cued-text presentation of the identical material. Since May 2003, there have been literally hundreds of academic contributions and developments in the field that are relevant to this research.

It would be safe to assume that as computer- and web-based technologies continue to hold a place in the development of the modern curriculum, scholarly interest in web-based instruction will endure. The keywords "online learning" and "research" in any scholastic medium will yield hundreds of references to the field. Due in a large part to the realization of anticipated accessibility to low-cost, wideband internet access, researchers continue to pay attention to the application of "best practices" to the available technologies.

Two articles in particular come from the *Journal of Online Interactive Learning*. This journal of theory, research, and practice in interactive online learning serves all disciplines and endeavors to provide a forum for the dissemination of research on interactive online education. They aim to disseminate ideas, further knowledge and understanding of emerging innovations and foster debate about the use and application of online education.

The aforementioned scholarly interest is evidenced in one particular review of online learning methods. Goldberg (2005) reviewed practices and processes for training faculty in the use of internet resources to build a hybrid or "blended" curriculum, combining aspects of face-to-face instruction with online learning. This study addresses a fundamental issue that I recognized in my 2003 study: The internet has indeed become a major element of the educator's toolbox. However, educators should be cautioned that poor course design cannot be saved by technology. Goldberg also affirms my assertion that modern application of online learning resources leans toward a more constructivist methodology. An underlying assumption appears—the design of web-delivered learning materials should be tailored to the type of material being taught. Goldberg identifies a potential flaw in common instructional design thought, specifically that the behavioral approach of teaching tasks is rarely addressed and only assumed as a prerequisite for using specific learning software.

Goldberg posits that the behaviorist approach, characteristic of Skinner's programmed teaching design of modeling and direct instruction, is recommended for teaching the technical areas of web-enhancing courses. The study then espouses a "project-based" progression into the course material. Implying a more constructivist methodology of "learning by doing." Goldberg suggests that faculty construct specialized web pages as project-based exercises to advance beyond the technical tasks learned through programmed instruction. Depending on the project and instruction, Goldberg infers that behaviorist educators could reason that this methodology is characteristic of guided practice. At least in part, the precepts of instructional design using programmed instruction, the basic contingency-response-feedback sequence are affirmed.

A second study, Chang and Ley (2006), is of particular significance. These researchers investigated the relationship between achievement and the quantity of online course materials that students printed and the frequency with which they reported using them. They addressed a significant factor in my study: That of experimental treatment integrity. Dividing their students into three groups: *Print, onscreen,* and *no preference,* this study found that onscreen preference learners had higher mean rank scores than print and no preference learners. There were no achievement differences between the online and hybrid learner groups. Learners who printed more preferred reading from printed online materials and experienced more onscreen reading difficulty than learners who printed less. In my study, students reported printing materials and using them for study prior to the computer posttest used for the evaluation.

It can be a difficult task, indeed, to account for individual study techniques and reading preferences. These factors must be addressed, however, in any experiments delivered in an uncontrolled environment over the internet. Chang and Ley (2006) tends to support my position that student study techniques could lead to potential problems of "treatment integrity" when experimental research is conducted over the web without supervision and insistence upon treatment delivery.

In my estimation, the enduring interest in the analysis of internet-based instruction shows that online learning remains an important area of research. I hope that this study proves itself beneficial to future research. Consistent with Cambria Press publishing policies, this work has complete documentation and methodology so that future scholars may build upon this work.

ACKNOWLEDGMENTS

The author wishes to thank those people whose invaluable assistance contributed to the completion of this volume. Appreciation goes out not only to those graduate students who participated in the study, but particularly to Mike Cohen, Darrel Davis, and "Gummi" Heimisson who personally supported this undertaking, putting in their personal time to help to gather the experimental data.

Thanks are especially extended to Dr. James White and Dr. William Kealy for their advice and inspiration. Gratitude is extended also to Dr. Stanley Supinski, a mentor, advisor, and friend.

Finally, this publication would not have been possible without the expert guidance of the author's esteemed advisor, Dr. Darrel Bostow. Not only was he readily available, as he so generously is for all of his students, but he always responded quickly and honestly to the myriad of issues that the author presented in the process of this endeavor. Although not a man of many words, his oral and written comments were always extremely perceptive, helpful, and appropriate.

Of course, despite all the assistance provided by Dr. Bostow and others, the author alone remains responsible for the content of the following, including any errors or omissions, which may unwittingly remain.

PROGRAMMED INSTRUCTION IN ONLINE LEARNING

INTRODUCTION

"I believe that consciousness is essentially motor or impulsive; that conscious states tend to project themselves in action." This excerpt from philosopher and educational theorist John Dewey's "My Pedagogic Creed" (Dewey, 1897) was later expounded upon in what could arguably be his most important work in the field of educational theory (Dewey, 1916). In "Democracy and Education," his assertion was straightforward. Students learn by doing. Empirical support for this assertion, in the context of active response during instruction, has been afforded by substantial and mounting research in education and behavior. Using both group-comparison and single-participant experimental approaches, researchers have come to the same conclusion: Learning is enhanced when the frequency with which students actively respond during instruction is increased (Bostow, Kritch, & Tompkins, 1995; Cronbach & Snow, 1977; Gropper, 1987; Kritch & Bostow, 1998; Kritch, Bostow, & Dedrick, 1995; Lunts, 2002; Rabinowitz & Craik, 1986; Rickards & August, 1975; Skinner, 1950, pp. 68–72; Thomas & Bostow, 1991; Tudor, 1995; Tudor & Bostow, 1991; Williams, 1996). In programmed instruction (PI), this active response allows the learner to control the advancement of the tutorial, incrementally progressing though the lesson material, and sequentially building up to the desired terminal behavior. "Learner control" in this behaviorist perspective is defined in terms of reinforced response to discriminative stimulus. This perspective holds that a student will learn as a result of being positively reinforced for having exhibited a specific observable behavior based on a particular contingent situation (Skinner, 1969).

Education in general, and the cited research in particular, has gone though an evolutionary progression. Programmed instruction grew from verbal and paper-based programs of study to teaching machines that provided automated instruction and facilitated learning by providing for immediate reinforcement, individual pace setting, and active responding. The emergence of technology in the last century and its continued advancement has broadened the perspectives of educational research. Studies using computer-based methods for delivering programmed instruction (Bostow et al., 1995; Kritch & Bostow, 1998; Kritch et al., 1995) have validated the significance of technology and its application in educational research and methods. A more recent influx in the field is the growing availability of high-speed, Internet-based distance learning. Despite these studies and the ostensible value of active learner response during instruction, much of what currently passes for computer- and web-based instruction does not use the basic contingency–response–feedback sequence. A learner can survey most web-based learning landscapes at his / her discretion "clicking" hyperlinks here or there, as desired, and advance to new material based upon his / her own criteria. Rather than progressing though a programmed course of material to focus the learner's attention on the desired behaviors, the student is allowed to follow his own interests, potentially skipping material that may seem uninteresting, to advance without complete understanding, and so on (Butson, 2003). Part of the reason for this could be that evaluation of a learner's performance on a web site is more difficult than in the traditional classroom environment. In the classroom, a teacher can observe student responses such as body language and facial expressions and provide more personalized instruction. This close student–teacher environment is a challenge to replicate in a web-delivered course. It is easier for instructional web designers to build educational material that is static and browsable rather than material that provides feedback, as well as adjusted stimulus, based on learner response.

Perhaps a more critical reason, however, for a passive presentation of lesson material may relate to the creator's philosophy of instruction. The role and importance of program-delivered instruction and correction is possibly not well understood or—of possibly greater concern—even discounted. It is argued, on the one hand, that the student must construct his own knowledge, while others maintain the control and guidance of the student in sequential, programmed steps of active response bring about more complete skills and capabilities. To date, these lines of reasoning have been tested and compared using paper-based lessons, teaching machines, and more recently, the computer-based methods of instruction. The advent of personal computing and the exponential growth of educational technology have generated many questions as to how the computer can supplement, improve, or perhaps replace established teaching methodologies. The internet is becoming a large part of the educator's toolbox. Web-based offerings in many academic disciplines are redefining the educational landscape and readily available high-speed access to the World Wide Web is shaping the field of distance learning. Kritch and Bostow (1998) studied the effect to which the degree of constructed-response interaction affected learning outcomes in computer-based programmed instruction. This study evaluated the importance of learner activity in computer-based programmed instruction. Four groups of undergraduate students experienced computer-delivered instructional programs, with varying degrees of interaction, which taught the use of a computer authoring language. Results revealed a clear superiority in both posttest and application performance with respect to those students who experienced the high density of active and meaningful participation. Performance of the passive group was the poorest. The present systematic replication was developed, in part, to substantiate the reliability and generality of the Kritch and Bostow (1998) findings. Contributing to mounting empirical data, this study extends the line of research in the field of "constructed-response inter-action" in computer-based programmed instruction.

This study, however, identified some potential deficiencies in Kritch and Bostow (1998) that helped to direct its development as a systematic replication. This study seeks to address the following questions:

- Are the results generalizable to different types of curriculum material?
- Did Kritch and Bostow (1998) account for the possibility of cueing in their high-density active group, compared to the text-based passive group?
- Would the technology available today, in terms of web-based instruction, have any effect on the results found by Kritch and Bostow (1998)?

To address the issue of generalization of the results, this study changed the subject matter content and type of the lesson material. Kritch and Bostow (1998) presented a lesson in computer programming. The level of abstraction of the material presented was analyzed by applying Bloom, Mesia, and Krathwohl (1964) taxonomy. While the outcome measures used by Kritch and Bostow (1998) tested the actual utility of the program produced by the participant students, the logical, sequential, and analytical skills needed for computer language programming are identified in the "analysis" category of Bloom et al. (1964) *Cognitive Domain*. At this level, the learner is able to assess lesson material in its component parts so that its organizational structure may be understood. This skill may include the identification of the parts, analysis of the relationship between parts, and recognition of the organizational principles involved. In contrast, the lessons presented in this study taught proper techniques for presenting data by way of graphing. Achievement of the terminal objectives was measured by the final product in the form of a hand-drawn graph, and results of a computer-administered test. While the levels of analysis and recognition were still in play for these lessons, incorporating aspects of comprehension from Bloom et al. *Cognitive Domain*, the particular spatial and manual skills requisite in drawing a graph from given data can be attributed to the third and fourth categories, "precision" and "articulation," of the Psychomotor Domain. At this level, skill has been attained. Proficiency is indicated by quick, smooth, and accurate performance, requiring a minimum amount of energy. The overt response is complex and performed without hesitation. In some cases the skills might be so well developed that the individual can modify movement patterns to fit special requirements or to meet a problem situation (Bloom et al., 1964). This study varied the type and category of the lesson material presented using the active and passive treatments. This was intended to expand upon Kritch and Bostow (1998) thereby generalizing the results to more varied academic disciplines.

In previous research, the comparison between active response and passive reading harbored a basic flaw. Participants who actively responded to instructional frames by "filling the blank" may have been inadvertently "cued" to the critical material in the lesson. The passive readers, however, had no point of reference or clue as to the critical material in their lessons. Answers to the posttest questions for students who had previously "filled the blank" might have been more easily recalled than by those who were not "cued" to the crucial material in the lesson. In this study, this issue of "cueing" was dealt with by a slight adaptation of the text-based, passive-treatment condition. This adaptation entailed the identification in the text-based materials of the key words and phrases by means of italicized text. The Publication

Manual of the American Psychological Association describes the appropriate use of italics to emphasize "a new, technical or key term or label." Thus, to overcome the possibly confounding variable of "cueing" in Kritch and Bostow (1998), this study afforded the text-based passive learning group "cues" by the italicized emphasis of the key words and phrases in the material.

The question of delivery method derived from Kritch and Bostow (1998) led this study to bring the lesson presentation up-to-date. The internet is the biggest, most powerful computer network in the world. It includes 1.3 million computers used by millions of people in over fifty countries. As connections to the internet have increased and availability of high-speed service has grown, educators have more possibilities to overcome time and distance to reach students. Distance learning is the "new frontier" of education. This study focuses and modernizes the question of constructed response and its effect on learning by presenting the lessons using the World Wide Web as the medium of delivery.

Two web-based tutorials, one using programmed instruction and the other using text and graphics-based web pages, were employed to deliver identical lesson content, teaching the methods of measuring, and graphically recording active human behavior. For this study, programmed instruction is defined as the use of technology to deliver educational course material in sequentially arranged contingencies of reinforcement. This process, using computer- and web-based apparatus, enhances the paper-based teaching machines of the late fifties and early sixties. After completing the online lessons, the participants' performance was assessed by directly observed, overt responses. The expected terminal performances for the tutorials in this instruction were (1) the appropriate selection from a variety of optional methods and visual arrays, (2) the formatting of data recording sheets appropriate to the behavior and setting, and (3) accurate selection of the proper recording method.

"Instructional Method" was the independent variable for this study. This variable had two levels—"active" Programmed Instruction and

TABLE 1. Description of the Independent Variable
(Instructional Method)

Instructional Method (Web Delivered)	Learner Participation	Lesson Advancement
Programmed instruction	Active	Program controlled
Cued-text and graphics	Passive	Learner controlled

"passive" Cued-Text and Graphics. Inherent in each of the two methods of web-based presentation are distinct levels of learner participation and control of lesson advancement. For the present experiment, programmed instruction represents "active" learner participation and "program advanced" lesson material. Learner participation in the Cued-Text and Graphics presentation is distinguished by "passive" reading of the lesson material and "learner advanced" lesson materials. Table 1 describes the relationship between the conditions, as well as the learner participation and lesson control assumptions in the independent variable.

To evaluate the relation between instructional method and performance, two dependent variables were identified in this study. Both dependent variables were assessment results. The first was a computer-based posttest that measured the student's retention of the lesson material, and the other was a learned skill application that appraised the student's ability to utilize the skill sets learned by actually assessing a set of data and presenting it graphically as taught by the lesson.

This research expounds upon theories of learning stemming from an experimental science. To make use of the rapidly growing field of web-based distance learning, the focus was to identify and validate a crucial component of interactive computer-programmed instruction. The study centered on a fundamental research question:

> In two types of web-based tutorials, distinguished by
> the existence of constructed-response contingencies, is
> there a significant difference in performance outcome,

based on learner participation, and the control of lesson advancement? Specifically, "Will teaching method be related to graded outcome on a computer-based test?" and, "Will teaching method be related to outcome on the graded results of an applied task?"

BACKGROUND

Science renders knowledge public through the application of experimental investigation, both quantitative and qualitative. In the field of educational research, this investigative study manifests itself as historical, qualitative, descriptive, correlational, causal-comparative, or experimental research. The scientific community self-regulates and provide for internal checks and balances by making use of processes such as peer review, cooperative research, journal publication and such appraisal mechanisms as meta-analysis and systematic replication. A systematic replication repeats or duplicates a previous experiment, varying a number of conditions, such as task, setting, or other parameters of the basic procedure. In systematic replication, the same hypothesis or hypotheses is tested again, using different participants and specific differences in methods. Obtaining similar results in the replicated study provides evidence of the generality of the original findings, by the principle of converging evidence (Durso & Mellgren, 1989; Kerlinger, 1986).

In this study, Kritch and Bostow (1998) are systematically replicated with variations in (1) the method of lesson delivery (lab computers vs. web-based presentation), (2) the type of learning involved in the lesson content (logical, sequential analysis skills needed for computer language programming vs. the spatial and manual skills requisite in drawing a graph from given data), and (3) the identification to the participants in both groups of key lesson concepts (overt, constructed response vs. passive, italicized cued-text). It should be mentioned that while not a specific modification of the previous study, the general technological background, in particular, computer literacy, of the participants in this study is conceivably higher. Computers and technology represent a paradigm shift in academic media; and today's students are increasingly more exposed to technology than students of only a few years past. This research is logically related, and imparted a different perspective into the experimental conditions undertaken in Kritch and Bostow (1998).

THE EXPERIMENTAL ANALYSIS OF BEHAVIOR

The approaches employed stem from lessons learned in an experimental approach to learning. They are based in what has been called "the experimental analysis of behavior," (EAB) a phrase coined by Skinner (1969, 1972) to address a specific category of the natural sciences. This category refers to the functional interactions between directly measurable behaviors and specific historical and immediate environments. The EAB presupposes that the formation and behavior of organisms are a result of natural selection, that is, evolutionary processes (Skinner, 1969).

According to the behavioral perspective, learning is identified as a permanent change in behavior due to experience or practice. The focus of this approach is on how overt behavior is affected by the learning environment (Huitt & Hummel, 1998). Predictable interactions between the behavior of living organisms and environmental variables are referred to as "functional relations." Johnston and Pennypacker (1980) describe a "functional relation" as the variation in responding that is a direct function of variation in a specific aspect of the environment. Not to imply a "cause and effect" association, but rather to demonstrate how observed environmental and behavioral events occur collectively in distinct ways under specific conditions.

In the experimental analysis of behavior, "behavior" is defined as "any directly measurable thing an organism does" (Sulzer-Azaroff & Mayer, 1991) and, Skinner (1969) characterized it as a measurable change in the status of an organism. For precise measurement, behavior must be identified objectively as an observable occurrence, open to thorough scientific analysis (Cooper, Heron, & Heward, 1987). Likewise stated, behavior is not a mere "expression" of other processes, rather a unit of measurement. "An emphasis upon the occurrence of a repeatable unit distinguishes an experimental analysis of behavior from historical or anecdotal accounts" (Skinner, 1969).

THE CONTINGENCY OF REINFORCEMENT

From the point of view of the EAB, the "contingency of reinforcement" is held to be the core of the process through which most practical behavior develops (Skinner, 1968). There are three variables that compose a contingency of reinforcement under which learning takes place. These variables are (1) an occasion upon which behavior occurs, (2) the behavior itself, and (3) the consequences of the behavior (Skinner, 1968). The term "contingency" was initially understood as something similar to "contiguously"—where events closely precede, follow, or coincide with another. However, an if / then, behavior / consequence, dependency is not necessary for the consequence to have a strengthening effect upon the behavior. All that is necessary is contiguous occurrence (Skinner, 1969).

In the process of operant reinforcement, precursor or concurrent stimuli attain the capacity to increase the likelihood of occurrence in the future. Laboratory research suggests that learning does not occur by merely watching or even performing, as Aristotle asserted; operant behavior is modified only when significant consequences are involved (Skinner, 1938). Simple execution does not determine behavior and make it more likely to occur again; "practice" on its own, does not "make perfect." The most apparent implication obtained from the operant laboratory is this: Strengthening, that is, the increased probability of future occurrence, calls for a behavior to both be emitted and then reinforced (Skinner, 1969).

To recapitulate, the experimental analysis of behavior presupposes that the basic building block of most of behavior is the "contingency of reinforcement." It is the key "learning unit" of the process of instruction (Skinner, 1968). The term "reflex" has never been a satisfactory means of expression to account for most behavior. Practical everyday behavior (which could arguably be called the motivation of nearly all instruction) is operant behavior, not respondent. The functional relations of operant behavior are those central to the process of instruction. Therefore, to skillfully develop behavior, the teacher must be able to correctly identify and arrange reinforcement contingencies (Skinner, 1968).

To be appropriately referred to as a "contingency," a situation must consist of the environment, behavior, and a strengthening consequence. Instructional technologies can be their most powerful when they present carefully arranged, sequential contingencies of reinforcement. Contingencies are deemed "programmed" when they are arranged in a tight, well-planned sequence. During this sequence, behavior is gradually strengthened and brought under the control of stimuli through the process of differential reinforcement of successive approximations. This organization of sequential contingencies is called "programmed instruction" (Skinner, 1968, 1969).

Educational practices have been greatly shaped by increased knowledge about operant conditioning. All learners exhibit behavior. Educators are, by definition, behavior modifiers as a result of their influence in the classroom. Behavioral studies in classroom settings have established methods to organize and arrange the physical environment and lesson presentation to produce desired academic behavior. Programmed instruction is one such method. Programmed instruction requires that learning be done in small steps, with the learner being an active participant (rather than passive), and that immediate corrective feedback be provided at each step (Huitt & Hummel, 1998).

PROGRAMMED INSTRUCTION

Programmed instruction, in the simplest terms, is a teaching technology that features educational practice resulting from laboratory and applied research in the area of experimental analysis of behavior. Some of the practice derived includes active student responding, priming, prompting, fading, and shaping. Educational content is said to be "programmed" when constructed, as Burton, Moore, and Magliaro (1996) quote Skinner, "of carefully arranged sequences of contingencies leading to the terminal performances which are the object of education."

As a teaching technology, PI has its roots in behavioral science, which is now entering its ninth decade (Burton et al., 1996). Developed from Skinner's "teaching machine" concepts, PI established its effectiveness across disciplines, and was once the preferred method for teaching. The evolution of so-called, cognitive learning theories has not boded well for the theories of behaviorism, being misrepresented and even excluded from contemporary programs of study. Programmed instruction has, however, been established as an effective method of instruction.

Boden, Archwamety, and McFarland (2000) reviewed 30 independent studies comparing programmed instruction to conventional teaching methods. Using meta-analytical techniques, Boden integrated the findings from these studies to make evident that programmed instruction results in higher student achievement. The primary focus of Boden's study was to find a correlation between class size and achievement. However, no significant correlation was found. Nevertheless, an increase was noted in the effect size for this study compared to a previous meta-analytical study. This increase was partially attributed to more effective use of programmed instruction in more recent years. The essence of the results of this study is that programmed instruction was more effective than conventional methods of instruction.

Despite many years of popular use and the continued improvement in the effectiveness of its application, programmed instruction has become an anathema to some. While getting a couple of conceptual details correct, Slavin (2000) appeared to misrepresent programmed instruction as an impractical approach to instruction. He expressed several points to identify PI as "self-instructional" and condemning it for establishing a setting where "students are expected to learn (at least in large part) from the materials, rather than principally from the teacher." And despite previous research into the use and effectiveness of PI, Slavin (2000) opined, "the programmed instruction techniques that were developed in the 1960s and 1970s generally failed to show any achievement benefits." Continuing his analysis, Slavin alleged "programmed instruction methods have not lived up to expectations …" and blamed the "expense and difficulty of using programmed instruction" as the reason why "this strategy is seldom used today as a primary approach to instruction."

Notwithstanding the potential influx of criticism from advocates of non-behaviorist approaches, Bostow et al. (1995) discussed the interaction of learners as being more significant in cases where the learner must "overtly" respond. This overt response, or behavior, is strengthened with successful interaction and results in increased motivation for student and teacher. These interactions involve "learning units" which are described in behavioral terms as reinforcement contingencies. Recognizing the evolution and expansion of computers in the classroom, Bostow et al. (1995) pointed out several areas where computers can make dramatic improvements, but emphasized the need for highly disciplined application of the various techniques of programmed instruction.

Referring to computers as "modern-day teaching machines," they pointed out that, while the computer is an instrument with the potential for delivering differential reinforcement in programmed instruction, software is developed for aesthetic and commercial appeal instead of tapping into the vast potential of these machines. Bostow et al. also suggested the use of computers as testing devices, to make test administration and scoring easier, and to improve the security of test information. Their conclusion was that the actual instruction itself could be accomplished by properly designed program of instruction. "Computers as teachers" can work if the programmer / teacher is not only well versed in the tenets of programmed instruction, but also possesses an understanding of a science of behavior. Programming the course content into effective programmed instruction allows the computer to "teach" and frees the instructor for direct student contact and mentoring.

To his credit, Slavin (2000) properly described the "learning units" mentioned above, identifying the reinforcement contingencies as "small subskills." Slavin went on to illustrate the frequent and immediate feedback associated with programmed instruction "so that students can check the correctness of their work," and conceded "similar approaches are quite common in computer-based instruction."

The concept of "overt response" or "active student responding" was studied more closely by Tudor (1995) in an experiment that evaluated the effects of overt answer construction in computer-based programmed instruction. This study incorporated practical application in addition to the statistical analysis of the data. Tudor pointed out that previous research had not generated convincing support for the need to use overtly constructed responses, citing issues with consistency of instructional programs across studies. Testing methods were also referred to, as well as program quality, and prior familiarity with subject matter. Tudor proposed, "the rules that might guide the designer of better instructional software cannot be easily extracted from past research." For this study, 75 students were placed into one of five groups to receive the programmed instruction, teaching the development of frames for PI, in varying levels of student interaction with the materials. All the groups showed significant improvement from pretest to posttest. The groups performed progressively better as the level of student interaction increased. The result being that this student interaction, be it in the form of overt or covert answer construction, resulted in a 13% better performance on a fill-in-the-blank posttest, and showed a better grasp of the concepts when later applied to constructing PI frames. Tudor pointed out that the differences were comparatively larger than in previous programmed instruction research and may have educational importance. The question raised addresses the functional significance of the behaviors that an instructional program is designed to produce. "Can teachers design frames that actually change behavior? In other words, can students use a washing machine correctly after completing a program?" Tudor recognized a need for future studies to identify "behavior change produced by interactive instruction." A significantly smaller sample participated in Tudor's (1995) study to isolate the effects of active responding in computer-based instruction. The four students in this experiment worked through a set of programmed instruction that alternated between frames with blanks that required overt answer construction and all-inclusive frames without blanks. Each student produced a higher percentage on posttest questions that corresponded to program segments that called for construction of overt answers. Regardless of the small sample, this study does confirm the importance of active responding in the effectiveness of instructional programs.

The "constructed-response contingency" could be associated to the "generation effect" studied in depth by Rabinowitz and Craik (1986). The generation effect suggests that verbal material that is actively generated (such as the overtly constructed-response) during the presentation of lesson material is later recalled more readily than material that is simply read. Study participants either read or generated target words in the existence of particular "generation" cues. The recall of the target words was studied using variation in the cues. In the instructional phase, when the target words were generated, prompted by associate related or rhyming cues, an observable generation effect was noted when the posttest used similar "retrieval" cues. This effect was not noted with weak relations between the cues and the targets. Semantic similarities between the cues and the targets did tend to yield an observable generation effect. Rabinowitz and Craik (1986) suggested that, as a result of direct guidance by an associated cue word, there was not only a strengthened memory of the generated target word, but also that the generation tended to enhance information specific to the cue–target relationship. The information used to guide the generation process for the learner is what is enhanced by generating, as compared to reading. This study substantiated the need for both associative and semantic origins of the cue words or phrases used in developing effective programmed instruction.

The word *interactive* has become a commercial selling tool for software developers and a selling point for hardware manufacturers. For the domain of educational technology, interactivity should refer to the behavior of the learner (Kritch et al., 1995). Kritch also addressed the theme of constructed response by learners using interactive computer-based instruction. In a double-pronged experiment, Kritch confirmed recent studies that identified the need for constructed answers in the application of instructional programs. This study confirmed the greater effectiveness of "constructed response" when compared to "click-to-continue" or "passive viewing formats," and corroborated Tudor and Bostow (1991) and Thomas and Bostow (1991). Using a second experiment, internal to the study, Kritch et al. (1995) upheld the findings of the first experiment using a counterbalanced (ABAB–BABA) design with a sample from each of the three groups from the first experiment, identifying high, moderate, and low ability students. Effectiveness in the first experiment was measured by posttest achievement by 101 college students. Not surprisingly, the achievement results for the constructed-response group were significantly different from the click-to-continue and passive observation groups. Results for the latter two groups were not significantly different. "Supplying missing words in frames required students to read more slowly, carefully, and to reread frames." Results of the second experiment in this study "confirm that active construction promotes recall and evidence indicates that programmed instruction is appropriate for all student ability levels" (Kritch et al., 1995). The study identifies itself as "a first step in the search for currently established (especially practical) functional relations." Indeed, prehaps it is a first step in getting the student to properly operate a washing machine through the use of programmed instruction.

Kritch and Bostow (1998) extended the available research and literature in the area of programmed instruction by revisiting the issue of functional relations among varying levels (densities) of constructed-response contingencies. About 155 undergraduate students were presented with a lesson in the use of a computer program authoring language, by way of programmed instruction at three levels of constructed-response contingencies, high, low, and zero, to which the students were randomly assigned. Student achievement was measured with a computer-delivered posttest, and also by an evaluation of practical application of the relevant applied skill (authoring program code). The students in the high-density condition produced higher achievement scores in both forms of assessment. The results of this study support the position that increased interactivity (as a function of student behavior) produces increased learning. The suggestion for future research advocates a closer examination of the relation between increased constructed-response contingencies and outcome measures by perhaps using a finer continuum of varying densities of "learning units."

The concept of programmed instruction has evolved and adapted since derived from the tenets of a science of behavior, nearly a century in the process. This concept has found new and effective application through the use of computer-based, and more recently, web-based instruction. The ongoing improvements in computer and communication technologies have opened new avenues for the precepts of behavioral analysis in education. This study endeavored to refine Kritch and Bostow (1998) by essentially replicating the conditions, using new lesson content with a new presentation medium, to evaluate the study's generality.

FEEDBACK

Examining how feedback functions within a wide variety of learning domains is the first recommendation offered by Morey (1996). Overt standards such as concept acquisition, rule use, and problem solving are identified as sources for researchers to explore. Unfortunately, this article on feedback research also charges the reader to analyze cognitive aspects such as learner motivations and attitudes, focusing on difficult to measure ideas such as "tenacity, self-efficacy, attributions, expectancy, and goal structure." Morey asserted, "no learning would occur unless some type of feedback mechanism was at work." He identified feedback as carrying out a crucial purpose in the acquisition of knowledge. Across the varied learning paradigms that the field of education has to choose from, feedback, as a part of instruction, remains a constant.

Azevedo and Bernard (1995) synthesized twenty-two studies in a meta-analytical analysis to investigate the effect of feedback in computer-based instruction. Azevedo and Bernard (1995) put forward that the concept of feedback as reinforcement in the stimulus-response model is now outdated, leaning toward more contemporary cognitive perspectives. This study did, however, concur with the idea that feedback is a critical component of instruction. Azevedo and Bernard cited variations in types of feedback ranging from "the very simple issuing of right–wrong statements," as presented in the programmed instruction condition of the current research, to more elaborate corrective statements. Adaptive feedback was also mentioned as a progression developed to adjust to the individual learning needs of students. The meta-analysis focused on the relative effectiveness of feedback in general, among various computer-based instruction environments. Four previous meta-analyses in the general area of feedback were identified, 1991, 1988, 1983, and 1982, only one (1983) examined the effects of feedback on learners in computerized and programmed instruction. It found a medium effect size of 0.47. Since this study included paper-based as well as computer-based instruction, Azevedo and Bernard give good reason for studying the pure effects of feedback in computer-based instruction with a new meta-analysis. The "new" meta-analysis, presented by Azevedo and Bernard, indicates an overall weighted effect size of 0.80 suggesting that achievement outcomes were greater for the feedback group than the no-feedback group. Concurring with Morey (1996) and sharing in the general consensus that feedback is one of the most critical components of Computer Based Instruction (CBI), analysis by Azevedo and Bernard found the higher performance of learner achievement was attributable to the large effect size for the feedback group. However, Azevedo and Bernard identify potential flaws in their analysis, due to the number of rejected studies. This "bespeaks the somewhat methodologically weak state of research in the area" (Azevedo & Bernard, 1995).

In general, the value of feedback cannot be overlooked in the design of computer-based instructional materials. Feedback can guide the learner through a tutorial, prompting correction, review, and in some cases encourage the motivation to successfully continue. As presented in the third leg of the S–R–R method, feedback offers the discriminative reinforcement necessary to shape learner behavior toward the objectives of the particular lesson.

LEARNER CONTROL

"Learner control," a concept that is readily described in terms of autonomy and independence, is generally defined as an instructional delivery system "where learners make their own decisions regarding some aspect of the 'path,' 'flow,' or 'events' of instruction" (Williams, 1996). After reviewing many analyses that compared learner control to program control in CBI, Williams pointed to the disappointing empirical findings that did not show learner control to be superior to program control in computer-based instruction. He later asked, "Can a comprehensive, integrative, deductive, prescriptive, and testable theory of learner control be developed?" His impression, that such a theory may not be scientifically disproved by a valid deductive argument, led to an alternative question. He suggested that we ask "whether we can still develop instructional prescriptions for the use of learner control which are at least pragmatic and are grounded in some reasonable psychological and educational principles." In this, Williams was optimistic and cited several reviews that indicate examples of application of the concept of learner control.

Perhaps not quite as optimistic is the critique presented by Reeves (1993) that puts forward the premise that learner control research is pseudoscience because, being contrasted to program control, it does not meet major theoretical and methodological assumptions, generally accepted in the research methodologies of the scientific, quantitative paradigm. Learner control is, in his characterization, a "design feature of computer-based instruction that enables learners to choose freely the path, rate content, and nature of feedback in instruction." Reeves cited poor definition of the concept of learner control. The definition seems clear and important, but it is so loosely defined in practice that the definition means very little. While clearly identified as a scientific construct, as a matter of scientific study, the concept of learner control must be well defined and readily measurable. Reeves also referred to the brevity of the instructional treatments used in various studies of learner control. Interaction time of 29 minutes 4 seconds, 29 minutes 6 seconds, were noted and other studies reported average treatment time of 25–30 minutes ranging as low as 13 minutes in the various presentation conditions, hypertext, computer-assisted instruction, programmed instruction, etc., where learner control was being studied. This Reeves contrasted to the guidance of Cronbach and Snow (1977) that ten or more separate interactive sessions were necessary to acquaint students with innovative instructional treatments. "How," Reeves asks, "can a dimension as complex as learner control be expected to have an effect in one-session treatments lasting less than an hour?" A second criticism of the research into learner control pointed to a lack of consequential or relevant outcome measures. He stated that the participants in learner control research should be engaged in education that is meaningful on a personal basis and has real consequences for them. He also addressed issues of small sample sizes and the concern over exclusion of participants who correctly answered all questions in the interactive session, raising the question as to whether the participant really "experienced" the treatment variables. Reeves did suggest some new directions. Primarily, he proposed that researcher and graduate students improve their understanding of contemporary scientific philosophy. This would expose us to a larger spectrum of approaches to scientific inquiry. He also suggested that researchers change the questions they are asking to determine why the field is not moving forward. Reeves noted, "without observations of the whole system of interrelated events, hypotheses to be tested could easily pertain to the educationally least significant and pertinent aspects, a not too infrequent occurrence" opining that such is the case of learner control research.

The disappointment in learner control theory was identified as a matter of definition and measurement of learner control by Lunts (2002) who published a very comprehensive review of learner control research. Lunts conveys the frustration in finding valid, reliable instruments to assess quantity and quality of learner control. He also acknowledged Reeves (1993) in the short duration of student exposure to the experimental treatments in various studies. Despite the brief encounters with the treatments, a few studies were mentioned that present a positive effect on achievement. The author warns, however, that the optimistic findings should be interpreted with caution, specifying the varying effects of content, sequence, and advisory control, which are the three major components of learner control. Studies were identified that make reference to intrinsic motivation and self-determination. Lunts' article actually classified learner control research into three primary categories: "Those that did not find any effect of learner control on students' motivation and attitudes toward learning, those that found a positive effect, and those that found a negative effect."

One of the studies identified by Lunts (2002) that did not find any effect of learner control on students' motivation and attitude was Cho's (1995) research studying the nature of cognitive processes that learners use under the conditions of learner-controlled and program-controlled environments. The qualitative aspect of the study, wanting for a scientific basis of measurement, was fuel for Reeves' position that learner control research is at best a pseudoscience. Regardless, the study collected student data on (1) a self-reported questionnaire providing data such as SAT scores, student experiences with *HyperCard* learning and lesson content knowledge, (2) audio and videotapes presenting participants' learning "behavior" during the *HyperCard* instruction, (3) recorded verbal data acquired from participants' think-aloud, stimulated recall, and interview data, (4) learning paths and time on task recorded by the *HyperCard* program, and (5) estimates of learning outcomes from the results of posttests. Cho (1995) indicated that learners' cognitive processes did not differ much between the learner control and the program control groups. It would be reasonable to imagine Reeves asking, "How exactly did you validate the measurement of the 'cognitive processes' of the participants in this study?" This study is representative of the perceived shortcomings of learner control research.

Perhaps in response to Ehrmann's (1995) call for a "guiding light" to piece together all the great ideas in educational technology, Molenda (2002) attempted to shine his light on *A New Framework for Teaching in the Cognitive Domain*. Combining the best of all worlds, Molenda identified programmed instruction, cognitive psychology, Gagné's (1985) events of instruction and constructivist influences to synthesize an inclusive framework that more unambiguously pointed toward the growing consensus that "meaning-making" (constructing?) is at the heart of cognitive learning.

The general impression garnered from the reviewed learner control research is that we need more standardization in measurement instruments. More importantly however, we need a standard by which to identify the aspects of behaviors that are valid, effective sources to measure learner control in the first place.

Textual Learning

Traditionally, in providing new information and curriculum material to students, texts have always had a very prominent place in education. The written word is a historical standard in teaching, and an accepted method of transmitting information. Siemens (2003) recognized text as the venerable backbone of learning. The majority of learners are quite comfortable with text-based learning, perhaps because of the many years spent using this medium. Table 2 summarizes the pros and cons of text as a teaching medium for the web (Seimens, 2003).

Text-based learning and memory retention based on isolation, the setting of a text item apart, has been studied at length (Cashen & Leicht, 1970;

TABLE 2.   Text as a Teaching Medium

Positives	Negatives	Use for Outcomes
Surveyable	Overused	Simple to complex
Easy to produce	Passive	Suited to synthesis / evaluation
Low bandwidth	100% learner motivation	Reflection—due to time lag
Familiar	Time lag	
Many readers		
Not much specialization		

Fowler & Barker, 1974; Rickards & August, 1975) in the academic setting. The Isolation Effect (Cashen & Leicht, 1970) indicates an improvement in item recall when text from a reading of course-related materials were set apart by underlining. Additionally, students retained material in the texts, adjacent to the highlighted materials, and showed a higher recall than students in the non-highlighted treatment tested on the same material. Fowler and Barker (1974) assessed the correlation between highlighting text as an alternative to typographical cueing (capital letters, italics, and colored fonts) to determine its effectiveness in improving retention. In this study, the experimenter highlighted (EHL) group performed slightly better than their control group (no highlighted material). The study concluded that highlighting, as well as traditional underlining, could produce improved retention of text material. Primarily studying the difference between student highlighting and experimenter highlighting, Rickards and August (1975) found that material highlighted by the students fell lower on the rating scale than those materials of high structural importance identified by the experimenter. Better student recall of experimenter-highlighted text was noted. Techniques used by the programmer (teacher) in the construction of educational material, to cue key information, can lead to better recall and improved learning. Wegner and Holloway (1999) posited that the role of the instructor becomes one of preparing the instructional environment, anticipating the needs of the students in advance and providing contingencies. They become Socratic questioners, resource providers, and motivators.

TYPOGRAPHIC CUEING

Learners can be motivated and provided resources through the use of cues in the text of instructional material. This is accomplished by using titles, headings, and subheadings, bold print or italics, captions, and other text features. Text-structure cues give learners insight into the organizational patterns and key information in various types of texts. Glynn, Britton, and Tillman (1985) reviewed studies on the effect of typographic cueing on learning. Typographic cueing, which generally refers to the use of bold or italic type or underlining, is used to signal the important ideas in a text. There is little doubt that this kind of cueing does work in focusing attention to the cued material. The consensus is that readers are more likely to remember cued ideas than uncued ideas (Hartley, 1987). Students who attend to textual cues are better able to comprehend, organize, and remember information presented in texts than those who do not (Manitoba Education, Citizenship and Youth, 2001).

Dyson and Gregory (2002) attempted to extend the existing research on text-based cueing to typographic cueing on computer-presented material. They identified that one of the underlying assumptions behind typographic cuing is that the cued material is more likely to be noticed by the reader. The general consensus emerging from the literature is that typographic cueing can improve the recall of cued material. Dyson and Gregory highlighted either key phrases or whole sentences that referred to main facts or incidental details in the lesson material. While the study did not find a significant difference between the experimental conditions and their control, there were differences in the various cueing conditions. These differences suggested that cueing an entire sentence can hinder overall recall, but cueing specific details is helpful.

Typographical cueing devices, such as font and color, help users assess the importance of the information they read and employ these keys in understanding and recalling the material. Within the content of a given lesson, the presented text is not a homogeneous structure in which all concepts have equal importance. The ideas often follow a pecking order and usually contain central and subordinate elements. Highlighting techniques (or directive cues), such as italics, color, or underlining, can draw the reader's attention to these key parts of the text. This typographic cueing can direct and guide the reader through the lesson material and contribute to the recall of key information (Allen & Eckols, 1997).

Headings, margin notes, or content markers, give structure and organization to the material. They also present a general organization to the text that helps the reader understand the content and coalesce new material with existing knowledge.

The Center for Learning, Instruction, & Performance Technologies at San Diego State University (Allen & Eckols, 1997) notes that the human eye is responsive to changing stimuli. Thus, boldface type set within a paragraph, or an italicized note within the text, will stand out from the rest of the display and draw the reader's focus. Thus, drawing the learner's focus meshes well with Gagné's (1985) suggestion that gaining the attention of the student is the first step in successful instruction.

COMPUTER-AND WEB-BASED INSTRUCTION

Computer-based and more recently, web-based instruction (CBI & WBI) has been incorporated and applied in many endeavors of transferring information for training and instruction. Realizing the web's full potential for learning is the vision of many educators. This realization is still hampered by various obstacles such as identifying appropriate pedagogical practices (Fisher, 2000) and overcoming the bandwidth bottleneck (Saba, 2000). With regard to evaluation, there has been an inclination for environmental comparison, such as the effectiveness of a technology relative to the conventional classroom (Wisher & Champagne, 2000). However, an appropriate assessment could be a comparison of the effectiveness of WBI to the historical findings on the effectiveness of conventional CBI. Unlike the fixed resources in conventional CBI, web-based instruction can be easily modified and redistributed, readily accessed, and effectively linked to related sources of knowledge. Compare these features to, say, an educational CD-ROM where content is encoded in its final form, availability was limited to specific computers, and immediate access to a vast array of related materials, as available through the internet, was not possible. Of course, key instructional features, such as learner control and feedback, are shared between web-based and conventional CBI. When well-designed instruction is coupled with computer delivery, the potential exists for improvement in learning.

"Behaviorism has had the greatest impact on the use of technology in education" (Thompson, Simonson, & Hargrave, 1996). However, the field of education has moved away from the behavioral approach and begun to focus on internal processes that take place in learners. The upsurge of technology development and application in the field of education is encouraging, yet the focus, to develop the most well-designed instruction may be veiled by a misunderstanding of the principles of Applied Behavior Analysis. "Constructivism" is the contemporary buzzword for ideas in educational research, theory, and policy (Duffy & Cunningham, 1996). Phrases such as "flexible navigation," "richer context," "learner centered," and "social context of learning," populate the literature on web-based instruction. Despite the proven and enduring nature of the behavioral approach in educational settings, proponents of this new paradigm of constructivism are quick to characterize any approach, other than constructivist as promoting passive, rote, and sterile learning. This shift puts a large stress on the issue of measurability since, by definition, the processes supposedly involved in constructivist ideas are internal and not readily observable. Mergel (1998) summarizes behaviorism, cognitivism, and constructivism and their histories in instructional design. "Eclectic" is a word used to describe the recommended approach to merging and applying the knowledge and insight garnered from each of the learning theories. This may be the first glimmer of the "guiding light" that Ehrmann (1995) suggests. The application of modern technology as a bridge between behavioral theory and ideas from the various new educational theories could perhaps be the first step in developing an effective, proactive method of course content presentation. The anticipated result is a sound approach, that when applied in the field of WBI, will benefit both the learner and the educator in terms of effectiveness and learner retention.

Much of the existing research in technology and education reflects an interest in multimedia environments. Increasingly, however, this research is focusing on the consequence of technology in education with studies that take into account diverse educational theories. Ehrmann (1995) sought to synthesize some of the research on technology in the classroom and concludes that one problem, ostensibly, is that individual efforts in the field of technology application can be quite effective, but for the educational community to benefit, there must be some "guiding light" to piece together all the great ideas. This light, or "roadmap," could give structure and direction to the blossoming efforts of many in instructional technology, a field that is developing in leaps and bounds. Both Clark (1983) and Kozma (1991) support the idea that some structure is appropriate, particularly to study which teaching / learning strategies are best (chiefly those not feasible without newer technologies) and which technologies are best for supporting those strategies.

THEORETICAL ASSUMPTIONS AND THEIR LINK TO SPECIFIC EXPERIMENTAL VARIABLES

Techniques for developing and shaping behavioral repertoires have been acquired and established by the application of the experimental analysis of behavior. It seems the crucial factor concerning these techniques is the presence of contingencies of reinforcement. Preceding research using text-based programmed instructional materials showed that learning takes place when what is emitted is subsequently reinforced (Holland, 1967). The instructional contingency (composed of stimuli that compel an overtly constructed response, upon which the learner receives immediate reinforcement for being correct) represents the essential juncture at which strengthening takes place. The research cited here (using computer-programmed instructional materials) has made evident the influential effects of instructional contingencies.

The experimental question is this: If the instructional contingency is indeed the critical factor in the learning process and in lab controlled computer-based instruction, and the existence of instructional contingencies has been previously shown to directly relate to how much or what is learned, is the process generalized to other mediums of learning and for other types of learning? To answer this question, the present experiment contained two versions of a web-based lesson. One was presented in a stringently controlled set of programmed instruction, and the other in a set of text and graphic-based web page presentations. Previous research using computer-programmed instruction has not compared these conditions using the World Wide Web as the medium for presenting the lesson content.

Reasoning for the Present Study: A Continuing Line of Research

Perhaps confusion about the instructional principles derived from the scientific analysis of behavior has prevented their widespread use in the field of instructional technology. If these procedures and techniques were clearly understood, developers of instructional programs could begin to make the most of computer- and web-based technologies to reinforce learner-constructed responses by applying pertinent knowledge of contingencies of reinforcement within computer- and web-based instruction. The field of instructional technology, and educational research in general, can reap benefits from the extended study of how contingencies of reinforcement and improved achievement are related. This research would, as its primary objective, investigate the practical relation between the learner's behavior and the method of delivery of lesson content. The present research was a follow up to the preceding review of germane literature, suggestions, and continued research in the field of computer- and web-based programmed instruction.

Foregoing research has made a strong case contending that the presence of instructional contingencies, entailing overt, constructed responses generates higher achievement as measured by posttreatment examinations. Additionally, such contingencies may produce an effective motivational environment. The available research that has endeavored to study the relation of constructed-response contingencies in computer-programmed instruction to practical implementation has also shown favorable results.

A significant difference in this study is the identification by italics, in the text and graphics-based treatment, of the key words or phrases that are identified in the Program Control Treatment. These key words and phrases were identified by the constructed-response contingencies in the programmed instruction tutorials. Identifying and emphasizing the key information in the passive treatment afforded the participants in that group the benefit of the retention and learning identified by previous research in isolation. By italicizing the salient words or phrases in the text and graphics-based treatment, this study generalized research in isolation and setting apart of text (Cashen & Leicht, 1970; Fowler & Barker, 1974; Rickards & August, 1975) to the typographical cueing inherent in italicized text. Although constructed responding has been previously compared to mouse clicking, key tapping, and passive reading, the specific contingencies (text or phrases) eliciting the constructed response have not been highlighted in the compared methods.

The purpose of the present experiment was to analyze the functional relation between constructed-response contingencies using web-based programmed instruction tutorials and two outcomes: (1) Achievement measured by a computer-based posttest and (2) the extent to which students can later apply the target skills. Using web-based media, the experiment compared the relative effectiveness of constructed-response, programmed instruction with passive reading of instructional materials. The research studied the correlation between learner "interaction" (overt, constructed responses elicited by instructional reinforcement contingencies) in programmed instruction and academic achievement. This extension of the existing research as a systematic replication stems from the emergent application of the World Wide Web as a teaching tool and offers a new perspective on the use of programmed instruction within the field of instructional technology. Besides including a traditional posttest evaluation and an applied performance measure, the study investigated the relation of several demographic characteristics of students with the research results using correlational analyses. The study included a survey to explore how participants viewed the instructional conditions and how they adhered to the plan of instruction for each treatment.

METHOD

PARTICIPANTS

One hundred forty-four graduate and undergraduate education majors from an educational foundations course at a large, state research university located in the southeastern United States served as participants. Programmed instruction was used to deliver all course content except for the lessons delivered in this study. Sixty-nine percent of the participants were female. The lessons presented in the experiment were a part of the course requirements and the students were advised that their participation would not have a detrimental effect on their class grade. Based on students, the lesson content was randomly assigned to experimental conditions by a computer program.

APPARATUS

The World Wide Web was used to deliver the instructional programs. Students could access the tutorials from anywhere they had access to the internet. Students were instructed to complete the lessons provided only, without note taking or printing of the materials for off-line study.

The instructional program used to present the programmed instruction was constructed using Practical Extraction and Report Language (PERL) version 5.8.3. PERL is Open Source software. It can be downloaded for free as a source code or as a precompiled binary distribution. PERL's process, file, and text manipulation facilities make it particularly well suited for tasks involving database access, graphical programming, networking, and World Wide Web programming. The instructional design principles and techniques prescribed for computer-based programmed instruction in the program called *Creating Computer Programmed Instruction* (Kritch & Bostow, 1994) were used to create the instructional program (see Appendix Twelve).

TREATMENT CONDITIONS

An 11-set instructional program about graphing data for behavioral analysis was developed prior to the conduct of this study. The content for these lessons was drawn from the text, Applied Behavior Analysis (Cooper et al., 1987) and used consistently throughout the two treatment conditions. These lessons were field-tested and revised using data from four graduate assistants in the Department of Psychological and Social Foundations.

The Constructed Response, Programmed Instruction Condition

The 11 tutorials presented in the program-controlled treatment contained 359 instructional contingencies, each providing a screen (see Appendix One) or "frame," of instructional material with one or more blanks to be filled in by typing an overt, constructed response at the keyboard. One hundred twenty-nine of these frames presented the user with a graphic image representing a particular relevant concept being taught by the lesson material. The PI program frames contained a total of 374 blanks within the 359 instructional frames, each requiring the student to supply constructed responses. Two hundred twenty-eight of these blanks contained formal prompt letters, and 120 blanks contained no formal prompting. Of the 228 blanks that contained formal prompting, 124 were discrimination frames that required the user to construct an echoic response. In other words, these frames provided alternative choices (within parentheses) that the user was to construct at the keyboard. Alternative choices were not represented by a symbol the user had to type, and hence were not considered to be traditional multiple-choice items. There were 17 frames that required only the typing of "true" or "false" for the lesson to proceed. Due to programming limitations, however, the PI program included nine traditional multiple-choice items in which at least two alternatives were presented. Here, the topography of the response involved typing a single letter symbol (e.g., a, b, c, etc.), which represented one of the alternative choices, instead of constructing an echoic, intraverbal, and overt response.

When a participant typed the correct response, the computer displayed "CORRECT!" in a green-colored font at the center of the screen and asked the user to "Press Enter or Click to Continue." The program then presented the next frame. If the answer given to a frame was incorrect, the program displayed "INCORRECT" in a red-colored font at the center of the screen, displayed the correct answer on the screen, and presented the student with a "Continue" button for the next frame.

The Passive Response, Cued-Text (CT) Condition
(see Appendix Two)

The second condition consisted of zero-density constructed-response presentations. Students experiencing this treatment were not required to overtly respond to any constructed-response contingencies. The material was divided similarly into 11 separate chunks each with identical lesson materials as the corresponding instructional set from the programmed instruction materials. The "chunks" were presented on

11 individual cued-text and graphics-based web pages with approximately 33 sentences per page. The lesson material was duplicated from the PI condition, but all blanks were filled in. The key lesson information, requiring a constructed response in the PI treatment, was typographically cued for the participants by the use of italics. Each word that represented the correct constructed response was presented in this treatment in italicized text to implement the desired cuing. Participants read each instructional set, arranged in the same linear order, with the identical corresponding graphics, but passively tapped the spacebar or clicked the mouse to return to the menu to select the next page. The pages for the instructional sets, however, could be seen in any order.

A 54-item fill-in-the-blank posttest of the lesson material and an application task were constructed to evaluate the degree of skills acquired by students in each of the treatment conditions. These answers were directly related to the key concepts taught by the instructional programs. Each posttest item evaluated a particular aspect of the lesson material whether on the nature of scientific data or the accepted rules for creating a graph suitable for journal publication. For example, " A second _____ axis is sometimes used to show different scales for multiple data paths." (The correct answer in this case was "vertical.")

The second dependent variable was the student's achievement in an applied task using the graphing skill learned from the lesson materials. This application of knowledge required the student to analyze a set of behavioral observation data, and given graph paper and pencil, represent the data series using the rules and structures learned in the tutorial.

PROCEDURE

To avoid exposure to the specific content of the lesson material, and potentially compromising the study by divulging key concepts before its initiation, a pretest was not included in the present experiment.

During the third week of class students in each of the four participating classes were randomly assigned to one of the two treatment groups. Each participant was individually notified of treatment assignment by e-mail (see Appendix Thirteen) through the course web site managed with WebCT. This e-mail correspondence included specific instructions and provided an internet link. Students were instructed to complete the tutorials for the lessons on "Graphing in Applied Behavior Analysis" during the fourth week of class. Each participant was scheduled for a two-hour appointment for a "Graphing Quiz" at the computer lab after the tutorial presentation week. Consideration was made in the schedule for the approximately 70 distance learners in the courses, allowing these students to choose a two-hour time frame during the week of testing. The schedule was posted in the "Bulletin Board" area of their course WebCT site. Assessment occurred from 11:00 A.M. to 4:00 P.M., the week immediately following the tutorial administration.

The random assignment was done using the original rosters from the first day of class. These rosters indicated a sample size of 232 students, however, after the first week of class, a number of students had exited the course through the university drop / add process. This attrition resulted in slightly unequal groups.

Students completed their assigned tutorials from the location of their choice, accessing them through the internet. Eighteen students reported that they had not been given a link to begin the graphing tutorials and after confirming their treatment group, the experimenter immediately sent a new notification e-mail to the individuals. The students proceeded as planned and 144 was the final tally of students completing the tutorials.

The following Monday, students began to report to the computer lab at their scheduled appointment times. The experimenter ushered each participant to a randomly assigned computer station and each participant was given a brief overview of the testing procedure. The participants were first administered a computer-based 54 question examination (see Appendix Three) of key concepts and material from the graphing lessons. The lab manager constantly monitored the computer lab throughout the testing phase of the experiment.

After completing the computer-based test, participants were directed to a separate classroom where another proctor administered the applied task assignment. A situation describing the gathering of particular behavioral data was given to each student. The proctor then presented each participant with a sheet of graph paper, pencil, and directions. Directions printed on the assignment asked each participant to assess the data and using the skills learned from the preceding lessons on graphing, make a proper graph(s) for the data presented (see Appendix Four).

The posttest consisted of 54 fill-in-the-blank items in a frame-by-frame presentation similar to the programmed instruction that all students were familiar with from quizzes on other course material. Validity of the testing instruments was endorsed by subject matter experts (SMEs), ensuring that knowledge of the lesson content was truly measured by the items of the test. Employing an objective approach to validation of the test, the SMEs utilized the text (Cooper et al., 1987) from which the lessons were created to compare and validate the test items. The representational acceptability criteria for each test item was derived from an analysis of the text content and used to assess the relevance and validity of each instrument. Both the computer posttest and the applied graphing task met the criterion derived by the SMEs for instrument validity. The computer posttest recorded each response, time taken to complete each item, and the percent correct score for each participant. However, students were not informed of their posttest scores (on either the product or computer test) to minimize post-experiment discussion with other students, and to avoid influencing participant motivation before proceeding to the applied graphing skill assessment.

To test for internal reliability of the computer-based posttest, the Kuder–Richardson 20 (Borg & Gall, 1989) test for internal reliability was calculated post hoc and yielded a score of 0.87. A 27-question rubric was designed to identify the required elements for the graphing assignment. To determine and maintain rater reliability for scoring the assignment, the service of an external assistant, unfamiliar with the graphing lessons, was enlisted. The assistant scored a random sample of 25 products using the product rubric sheet and key (Appendices Five and Six). The scores were compared with those of the experimenter who scored products using the identical product grade sheet and 100 percent agreement occurred. The assistant then scored every tenth product yielding the same agreement. The rubric was clear and explicit requirements were specified to identify key aspects taught in the lessons.

The Kuder–Richardson 20 test for internal reliability was also calculated post hoc for items on the applied task rubric and a reliability coefficient of 0.85 was obtained. Upon completion of the applied graphing assignment, participants were administered the post-tutorial questionnaire (see Appendix Seven). This questionnaire attempted to assess student attitudes regarding the experiment, their computer skill, and satisfaction with their method of instruction. The questionnaires were anonymous with the exception of treatment group identification. As a follow-up, five additional questions were asked of the participants via an online survey using the capabilities integral to the WebCT course management software (see Appendix Eight). These questions were posed to validate the results from the initial questionnaire.

Because appointments were scheduled at the same location throughout the week, discussion between students was anticipated. Therefore, each participant was given a "debriefing" immediately after completing the computer-based test. This interaction briefly described the importance of conducting educational research, asking participants not to discuss the experiment until results were provided.

EXPERIMENTAL DESIGN AND DATA ANALYSIS

One-way analysis of variance (ANOVA) was employed to evaluate differences in computer-based posttest scores and applied graphing products resulting from the experimental comparison conditions (Borg & Gall, 1989). A multiple analysis of variance (MANOVA) was also performed to assess the interaction between the two dependent variables (computer posttest results and applied task results) across the two independent variables (PI condition and Cued-Text condition). The MANOVA, however revealed no interaction effects among the variables ($p > F$:<0.0001).

Data for evaluation came from the PERL program which recorded percent correct scores on the computer posttest, the applied graphing rubric-scored products, and the questionnaires administered after completing all lesson and evaluation materials. Data records were assembled into summary charts used for the SAS statistical program. Table 3 summarizes the experimental conditions, response contingencies, and stimuli presented to the two independent variable groups.

TABLE 3.   Summary of the Experimental Conditions

Programmed Instruction Treatment (Constructed Response)	Cued-Text Treatment (No Constructed Response)
Overt responses to all frames, program advanced	Passive Web-page reading, advanced at student discretion
11 total tutorials	11 total Web pages
359 total frames	359 total frames (sentences)
374 total blanks	0 total blanks
359 frames requiring overt responses	0 frames requiring overt responses
228 blanks w/formal prompting	
124 discrimination frames	
104 partial word prompt	
120 blanks w/o formal prompting	
9 multiple-choice frames	
17 true–false frames	

RESULTS

Results of the ANOVA on posttest scores revealed significant differences between groups, $F(1,142) = 5.67$ and $p = 0.0186$. Table 4 presents ANOVA results and posttest means for the instructional conditions. In all statistical comparisons, a minimum alpha level of 0.05 was applied in assessing statistical significance.

Distributions of the posttest scores for each group are illustrated in Figures 1 and 3. The scores on the posttest for the PI group ranged from 83.3% to a low of 7.4%. Scores for the Cued-Text group ranged from a high of 79.6% to a low of 11.1%. Box and whisker plots in Figure 2 indicate the positive relationship between exposure to lesson materials requiring constructed responses and participants' performance on the posttest. The PI group had a higher mean score ($M = 40.85$, S.D. = 17.62), than the CT group ($M = 34.45$, S.D. = 14.61) programmed instruction, supplying contingencies of reinforcement that require overt constructed responses, is shown to be associated with higher posttest percent correct scores. These results were analyzed using a software-based tool (Devilly, 2004).

TABLE 4. ANOVA and Means—Computer Posttest

| Source | DF | Squares | Mean Square | F Value | p > F | Level of Treatment | | Computer Posttest | |
							N	Mean	S.D.
Model	1	1473.92063	1473.92063	5.67	0.0186	1	69	40.8521739	17.6234103
Error	142	36919.79937	259.99859	–	–	2	75	34.4480000	14.6121234
Total	143	38393.72000	–	–	–	–	–	–	–

FIGURE 1. Distribution of Computer Posttest Scores (PI Group)

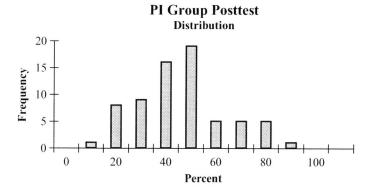

FIGURE 2. Box Plots of Computer Posttest Means

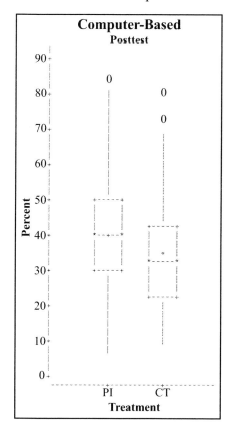

FIGURE 3.   Distribution of Computer Posttest Scores
(Cued-Text Group)

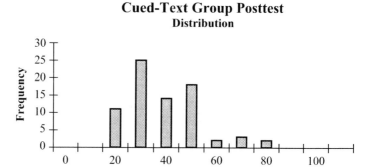

Cued-Text Group Posttest
Distribution

Results of the ANOVA calculated from the applied graphing scores did not reveal significant differences between groups, $F(1, 142) = 0.01$, $p = 0.9206$. Table 5 presents the ANOVA results and product score means for the two instructional conditions. The programmed instruction group produced means ($M = 51.10$, S.D. = 18.59) nearly identical to those produced by the Cued-Text group ($M = 51.41$, S.D. = 18.21).

The PI group scores on the applied graphing task ranged from a low of 3.7% to a high score of 85.2%. The Cued-Text group scores ranged from 7.4% to a high of 81.5%.

The near identical result in performance between the two treatment groups on the applied graphing task is represented by box and whisker plots in Figure 4.

Distributions of the applied graphing task scores for each group are illustrated in Figures 5 and 6.

The post-questionnaire consisted of 15 questions. The first two were for group identification only. Questions 3–15 were categorized as follows:

Questions 3, 7, 11: A—Personal assessment of computer skills.
Questions 4, 8, 12: B—Satisfaction with teaching method.

TABLE 5. ANOVA and Means—Applied Graphing Task

							Applied Graphing		
Source	DF	Squares	Mean Square	F Value	p > F	Level of Treatment	N	Mean	S.D.
Model	1	3.37206	3.37206	0.01	0.9206	1 (PI)	69	51.1043478	18.5849436
Error	142	48018.72016	338.16000	–	–	2 (CT)	75	51.4106667	18.2073313
Total	143	48022.09222	–	–	–	–	–	–	–

FIGURE 4.   Box plots of Applied Graphing Task Means

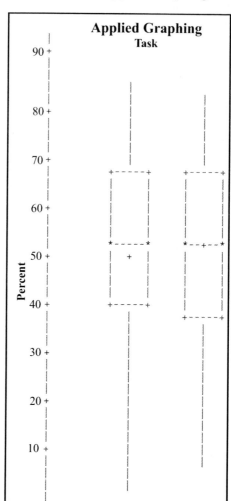

Questions 5, 9, 13: C—Personal assessment of learning environment.

Questions 4, 8: D—Personal assessment of reading / retention skills.

Questions 14, 15: E—Personal assessment of adherence to tutorial instructions.

FIGURE 5.   Distribution of Applied Task Scores (PI Group)

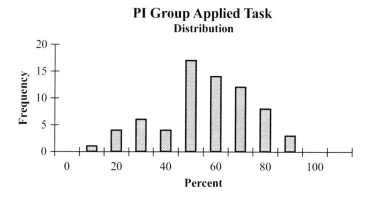

FIGURE 6.   Distribution of Applied Task Scores (Cued-Text Group)

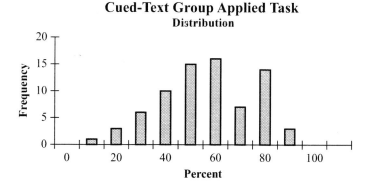

The graph in Figure 7 indicates the relationship between the treatment groups among the question categories. The largest difference between the treatment groups (0.8 for the Cued-Text-based group and 1.3 for the programmed instruction group) was in "Satisfaction with Teaching Method." Self-reported non-compliance with tutorial instructions was distributed throughout the two groups (16/67 in the PI group and 25/66 in the Cued-Text group). A post hoc analysis for relationships of the questionnaire responses yielded a χ^2 of 0.0344 and a correlation factor of 0.0354. While the plotted responses to questions in Category B

FIGURE 7.   Questionnaire Responses by Treatment

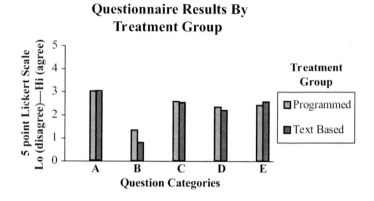

FIGURE 8.   Follow-up Questionnaire Responses

Follow-up Questions	PI	CT
1 – Tutorials only – no additional studying? (1 – Yes 2 – No)	1.2	1.3
2 – Confidence in graphing ability after tutorial? (Lickert: 1 = low 5 = high)	1.6	1.4
3 – Did you work with a partner? (1 – Yes 2 – No)	1.9	2.0
4 – Programmed Instruction or Text Based? (1 – PI 2– CT)	1.0	2.0

5 – Preferred instructional format?
  (Tally)

	PI	CT
PI	10 (15%)	26 (39%)
Web Text	18 (27%)	3 (5%)
Lecture	26 (39%)	24 (35%)
Group Study	6 (9%)	6 (10%)
1–on–1 Tutor	7 (10%)	7 (11%)

6 – Narrative expounding upon
  Question 1 [Appendix 9]

indicated a possible significance, the post hoc analysis revealed little or no real evidences against the indication of a relationship between the questionnaire variables.

Results from the follow-up questionnaire yielded similar results between treatment groups as indicated in Figure 8. Seven participants, five from the programmed instruction group and two from the Cued-Text group, indicated on Question #2 that they studied with a partner during the tutorial presentation phase. One participant, from the Cued-Text group, indicated on Question #3 that he or she found a way to experience both treatments. Fifty-six participants indicated they did additional studying for the graphing lessons with their response to Question #1 of the follow-up questionnaire (Appendix Eight). They elaborated with their responses to Question #6. The narrative comments are included (Appendix Nine) for those participants who indicated that they did some form of additional studying, besides completing the assigned lessons, and outside the scope of the instructions for the experiment.

DISCUSSION

The existence of constructed-response contingencies in web-based instruction is related to higher achievement on computer-based posttests. This finding generalizes previous results in the area of computer-based instruction to the delivery medium of the World Wide Web. These results contribute to the line of research that has identified a correlation between active, overt responding, and higher achievement. Additionally, the results generalize some findings of Kritch and Bostow (1998) to course content that falls in a different category and domain of Bloom et al. (1964) Taxonomy. Although the performance task, administered to each group in the form of a computer-based posttest, was verbal (Gagné, 1985) information / knowledge level (Bloom et al., 1964), the value of the constructed-response contingency was validated for a verbal information (Gagné, 1985) / knowledge (Bloom et al., 1964) level outcome measure.

The results did not prove as conclusive, or as supportive of previous research when the measure was based on student achievement on the applied task. Without a statistically significant difference between the treatment groups, the results of this study, as applies to student achievement on an assignment of practical activity, do not support Kritch and Bostow (1998). Initial analysis would suggest that Cued-Text in the non-programmed instruction treatment might be the likely explanation for the undistinguished findings. For all study participants, the lesson materials for the entire course, other than the graphing lessons for the Cued-Text group, were presented using programmed instruction. To mitigate the possibility of the PI group being exposed to a practice effect, the format of the questions delivered in the test instrument was significantly different than that of the tutorials. Test questions were terse with less cuing, requiring a higher level of recall for the graphing lesson content. It is noted that under the conditions of this study, based on the marginal to poor scores on both the posttest and the applied task, the treatments seem to have failed to teach proper graphing technique. This fact may be explained by the possibility of treatment novelty or participant uneasiness with the method of delivery of the testing instruments. Future studies should attempt to mitigate these possibilities by familiarizing the participants with the presentation method. Additionally, quizzes covering nonrelated material could be presented in the same format as the study testing instruments.

LIMITATIONS OF THIS STUDY

Of concern to the experimenter in the present research is that nearly 40% of the participants admitted to doing additional study while experiencing the treatments for the experiment. Whether the student printed off screens while going through the material, took notes, or studied with a partner, the additional study potentially contaminated the validity of the treatment conditions for those individuals. The potential could have existed for removing those specific individuals from the study, citing a compromise to treatment integrity. This idea was abandoned when the questionnaires were identified as anonymous and could not be related to a specific student. In any case, having random assignment for this study, the lapse in treatment integrity is assumed to have been randomly distributed throughout. Specifically, since self-reported non-compliance with tutorial instructions was distributed throughout the two groups, it is also assumed that the differences realized in the evaluations is not related to this implied "cheating."

The present experiment has identified a potential problem for research, particularly in the administration of treatment conditions by use of the World Wide Web. The nature of the medium, and the varying preferences of individual students, with regard to study habits, makes it difficult, if not impossible to control a web-delivered treatment. It could be argued that the treatment might be supervised, presented in a laboratory setting or somehow administered in a contrived control situation that forces the participants to participate exactly as the experiment specifies. This artificial control removes the students' option for exercising any supplemental study skills and paints a sterile, inaccurate picture of web-based learning. If we control the options of our participants in our research, what external validity will our research have when compared to how students "really" do it? This may bring into question the external validity of treatments using laboratory controls in web-based experiments.

IMPLICATIONS OF THIS STUDY

This study identified several lessons for application in future use of the World Wide Web as a medium for delivery of experimental treatments. Researchers would do well to increase the focus on developing research treatments that are more effective. Students tend to perform better in learning environments that they are comfortable with, enjoy, and have confidence in. Additionally, analysis of the questionnaires indicated that fifty-six participants found some way to supplement the lesson material that they were provided in the present experiment. It would be of value to consider the control issue regarding treatment integrity when choosing the web as the delivery tool. This must be weighed against the risk of establishing situations of "contrived" control in the name of treatment integrity. The World Wide Web is a dynamic medium, allowing learners much leeway in applying previously conditioned behaviors in the process of learning. Placing artificial limits on student activity may give the results we seek, but not accurately represent the environment that the student will actually be experiencing. The present research has also identified two major points of method that are worthy of mention:

1. Survey data may have proven more applicable had there been a way to associate a particular questionnaire to a specific participant. Identifying the students who admitted to going outside the treatment requirements may have allowed the experimenter to remove those students and the results might have been markedly different.

2. The World Wide Web is a newer medium for education and as an increasing number of classes and coursework is administered this way, researchers are going to adapt to a certain lack of control over the variable of treatment integrity. Students are going to do what they feel comfortable with in the process of studying. The present experiment validates this.

SUMMARY

This study indeed demonstrated a statistically significant difference in one of the dependent variables. However, the numbers may not accurately reflect the contribution of the independent variable in the treatment to the performance of the participants on either the computer posttest or the applied graphing task. While programmed instruction students performed better than the text group on a computer posttest, they failed to perform better on an applied graphing assignment. The results of the post-tutorial questionnaires revealed that a large number of students printed screens and took notes—studying these materials immediately prior to the computer posttest and applied task. This research draws attention to the potential problem of "treatment integrity" when experimental research is conducted over the web without accompanying supervision and insistence upon treatment delivery.

APPENDIX ONE

SCREEN CAPTURE—PROGRAMMED INSTRUCTION

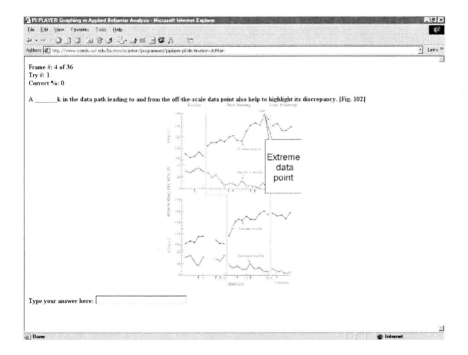

APPENDIX TWO

SCREEN CAPTURE—CUED-TEXT WEB PAGE

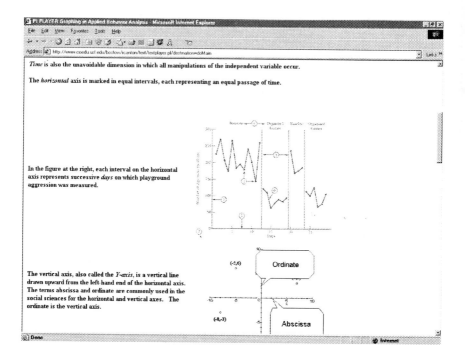

Time is also the unavoidable dimension in which all manipulations of the independent variable occur.

The *horizontal* axis is marked in equal intervals, each representing an equal passage of time.

In the figure at the right, each interval on the horizontal axis represents successive *days* on which playground aggression was measured.

The vertical axis, also called the *Y-axis*, is a vertical line drawn upward from the left-hand end of the horizontal axis. The terms abscissa and ordinate are commonly used in the social sciences for the horizontal and vertical axes. The ordinate is the vertical axis.

APPENDIX THREE

POSTTEST QUESTIONS

Graphs _____ information.
   [communicate]

_____ is indicated by the horizontal axis.
   [Time]

Stretching the ordinate serves to _____ the appearance of an experimental effect.
   [Magnify]

A vertical line on a cumulative record indicates a _____.
   [Reset]

There are _____ coordinates on a Cartesian plane.
   [two]

Vertical lines indicate _____ in experimental conditions.
   [changes]

A mean without raw data gives no evidence _____ in the experimental data points.
   [variations]

A _____ graph is better for showing differences in non-continuous data points.
   [bar]

A _____ graph contains more than one data path for subjects, situations, or behaviors.
[complex]

A slope is _____ when the rate is higher.
[Steeper]

A bar graph _____ presentation of variation.
[sacrifices]

When the target behavior is one that can occur or not occur only once per observation session, the effects of any intervention are _____ to detect on a cumulative graph.
[easier]

The data from multiple _____ are often stacked vertically within a graph.
[individuals]

The _____ is the average of a set of data points.
[mean]

A scale break is used to indicate _____ in the progression of time on the horizontal axis.
[discontinuity]

The purpose of a graph is to highlight _____ _____.
[functional relationships]

The vertical graphing of behaviors or situations is to determine whether changes in one variable are _____ _____ changes in other.
[accompanied by]

Depiction of data on a Cartesian plane is called a _____.
  [graphic]

Something systematically manipulated by the researcher is called the _____ _____.
  [independent variable]

A sequence of plotted data points is called a _____.
  [path]

Abbreviations can cause _____.
  [confusion]

The heart of behavior analysis is the _____ measurement of behavior.
  [repeated]

Visual analysis is a _____ method of data analysis.
  [conservative]

The scaling of the vertical axis should be _____ when small numerical changes in behavior are not socially important and the variability obscured in such a scale is not a significant factor.
  [contracted]

In applied behavior analysis, behavior is monitored _____.
  [continuously]

_____ is something an individual does.
  [behavior]

In the school bus study, both the _____ of disruptions and their total duration in seconds for each bus trip were plotted against the same vertical axis in this figure.
  [number]

Labels should be _____ but descriptive.
   [brief]

Labels identify _____ conditions.
   [experimental]

Major treatment changes are separated by _____ vertical lines.
   [solid]

Ordinarily _____ _____ range of possible values are indicated on the vertical axis.
   [the full]

Discontinuities in the time context should be clearly marked by _____ breaks.
   [scale]

The _____ _____ should also contain an explanation of any observed but unplanned events that may have affected the dependent variable at specific times of the study and should point out any potentially misleading or confusing features of the graph.
   [figure legend]

In applied behavior analysis, graphs provide _____ access to the original data.
   [direct]

In behavior analysis, behavior is the _____ variable.
   [dependent]

Minor experimental manipulations are separated by _____ vertical lines.
   [dashed]

The intersection to two axes is called the _____.
[origin]

Graphing one's own performance can be an effective _____.
[intervention]

_____ are printed beside and above a graph.
[labels]

The x-axis is a _____ line.
[horizontal]

"Data" in behavior analysis mean _____ results.
[quantitative]

In multiple-tier graphs, equal distances on each vertical axis should represent equal changes in behavior to aid the _____ of data across tiers.
[comparison]

_____ _____ are desirable when the total number of responses made over time is important or when progress toward a specific goal can be measured in aggregated units of behavior.
[cumulative records]

Graphs communicate without a _____ analysis.
[statistical]

In contrast to statistical evaluation, visual analysis imposes no predetermined or arbitrary level for evaluating the _____ of behavior change.
[significance]

Stretching or compressing the ordinate results in _____ of the data.
   [distortion]

Variability is more conspicuous with an _____ _____ graph.
   [equal interval]

The connecting step in the progression of successive applications of the treatment is called a _____ _____.
   [dog leg]

The line graph is based on a Cartesian plane, a two-dimensional area formed by the intersection of two _____ lines.
   [Perpendicular]

_____ labels identify the different conditions within a phase.
   [subordinate]

An "overall" response rate is the _____ rate of response over a given time period, such as during a specific session, phase, or condition of an experiment.
   [average]

The term semi-logarithmic chart refers to graphs in which only one _____ is scaled proportionally.
   [axis]

The rate within a narrow range of time is called the _____ rate.
   [local]

_____ data paths are also used to facilitate the simultaneous comparison of the effects of experimental manipulations on two or more different behaviors.
   [multiple]

A sequence of connected measurements is called a _____ _____.
   [data path]

In applied behavior analysis a _____ dimension of behavior is measured repeatedly.
   [quantifiable]

A graph is an easily understood presentation of the degree and nature of the _____ of behavior to an environmental variable.
   [relation]

The Standard _____ _____ provides a standardized means of charting and analyzing change in both absolute and relative rates of response.
   [behavior chart]

On most graphs the vertical axis can be drawn approximately _____ [include the hyphen in your answer] the length of the horizontal axis.
   [two-thirds]

_____ _____ make the comparison between very high rates difficult.
   [cumulative graphs]

An appropriate _____ _____ can be used to give the impression that changes are more important than they really are.
   [scale break]

The instructional decision-making system, called _____ _____ assumes that (1) learning is best measured as a change in response rate, (2) learning most often occurs through proportional changes in behavior, and (3) past changes in performance can predict future learning.
   [precision teaching]

An instructional decision-making system, called Precision Teaching, has been developed for use with the _____ _____ _____. This figure is an example.
    [standard behavior chart]

A scientific analysis evaluates the relation of behavior to its surrounding environment It targets some behavior and manipulates a (n) _____ variable.
    [independent]

When two data sets travel exactly the same path, the lines should be drawn close to and _____ with one another to help clarify the situation.
    [parallel]

Experimental changes are labeled at the _____ of a graph.
    [top]

_____ is the frequency of responses emitted per unit of time, usually reported as responses per minute in applied behavior analysis.
    [rate]

The figure legend is a _____ statement.
    [concise]

The _____ of a data path indicates the rate of behavior.
    [slope]

The vertical axis, also called the _____-axis [include the hyphen with the word axis].
    [Y]

When more than three data paths are displayed on the same graph, the benefits of making additional comparisons are often outweighed by the _____ of too much visual "noise."
   [distraction]

Unplanned events that occur during the experiment or minor manipulations that do not warrant a condition change line can be indicated by placing small arrows, _____, or other symbols next to the relevant data points.
   [asterisks]

When the same manipulation of an independent variable occurs at different points along the horizontal axes of multiple-tiered graphs, a dog-leg _____ the change lines of adjacent tiers makes it easy to follow the progression of events in the experiment.
   [connecting]

A label should be _____ along the y-axis.
   [centered]

In this figure, _____ change lines are drawn to coincide with the introduction or withdrawal of organized games.
   [phase]

With a graph you can use your eyes when presented in a format that _____ displays the relationships among a series of measurements, the meaningful features of a set of behavioral data are more immediately apparent.
   [Visually]

APPENDIX FOUR

APPLIED GRAPHING ASSIGNMENT

Your name: _____
Date: _____
Your class: _____

Graph this:

Two different troublesome children in separate classrooms were brought to your attention. The children engaged in TANTRUMS that totally upset the decorum of their two respective classes. You are the behavior analyst asked to help.

To obtain a BASELINE, you visited the FIRST classroom each day at the same time--the time that tantrums were exhibited most frequently (which was 11:00-12:00 AM).

You obtained a baseline on the SECOND child's performance during the very same school days, but from 1:00-2:00 in the afternoon. You observed from a corner of the rooms for one hour in each classroom.

During the first five days in the MORNING ROOM you counted the number of tantrums during each daily hour session.

You attempted to control the TANTRUMS in the FIRST classroom beginning on day 6. You suggested to the teacher that for the next few days, he, personally, very carefully avoid paying any attention to tantrums when they occurred.

(However, for comparison purposes, on these same-days you continued to record the baseline measurement of the child in the 1:00-2:00 room.)

Not being pleased with your failure to bring TANTRUMS under control in the first class by simply stopping teacher attention, you then suggested that he, in addition, prevent the other students from paying attention to tantrums (I.e. NO CLASS ATTENTION) for the next few days.

(But you kept the BASELINE condition running in the afternoon situation for all the same days as above.)

You were finally successful in the first classroom. Since the NO CLASS ATTENTION treatment reduced the tantrums in the first class, you also tried it in the second class.

Your data look like this:

MORNING CLASS (BASELINE: 11, 13, 12, 9, 13)
(NO TEACHER ATTENTION: 9, 15, 18, 7)
(NO CLASS ATTENTION: 8, 5, 0, 0, 0)

AFTERNOON CLASS (BASELINE: 8, 16, 40, 11, 5, 18, 13, 11, 12)
(NO CLASS ATTENTION: 9, 7, 3, 0, 0)

Graph these data using the all rules you learned in the tutorials you experienced.

You may have as much time as you wish.

If you need another piece of graph paper, ask for it.

The lab monitor cannot answer any questions about clarification of this assignment--simply do your best.

Appendix Five

Rubric for Applied Graphing Assignment

SCORING RUBRIC – SKILLS APPLICATION (GRAPHING)

1. Are there two graphs drawn?

2. Does the word "tantrums" appear sideways along the ordinate?

3. Does the word "morning" appear to the left of a graph?

4. Does the word "afternoon" appear to the left of a graph?

5. Is there an indication of the 11:00 to 12:00 session time anywhere near a graph?

6. Is there an indication of the 1:00 to 2:00 session time anywhere near a graph?

7. Is there a vertical axis for the graph(s)?

8. Is there a graph that shows three separate conditions along the horizontal axis?

9. Is there a "0" at the bottom end of the ordinate in the graph(s)?

10. Are the values along the ordinate evenly spaced and numbered in the graph(s)?

11. Is the line drawn as the horizontal axis slightly below the "0" point of the ordinate for the graph(s)?

12. Are the data points on the graph(s) slightly larger than the connecting lines?

13. Is the word "baseline" written as a horizontal label above this condition in the graph(s)?

14. Are the words "no teacher attention" written as a horizontal label above the appropriate data points in the graph(s)?

15. Are the words "no class attention" written as a horizontal label above the appropriate data points in the graphs(s)?

16. Is there a solid vertical line separating baseline from the other condition(s) in the graph(s)?

17. Is there a broken vertical line separating "no teacher attention" from the "no class attention" conditions in the graph(s)?

18. Does the data path for "no teacher attention" generally approximate the corresponding data path in the key(s)?

19. Does the data path for "no class attention" generally approximate the corresponding data path in the key(s)?

20. Does the data path for "baseline" generally approximate the corresponding data path in the key(s)?

21. Is there a "dog leg" showing the temporal offset of baseline termination in the graphs?

22. Is there a break in the data path that goes to the "40" data point in a graph?

23. Is the number "40" anywhere near the extreme data point?

24. Are the data paths in the graph(s) broken between experimental conditions?

25. Does the label "days" appear at the bottom of a graph?

26. Do the horizontal axes begin with a "0" at the left?

27. Is there at least one pip and an appropriate number below it on the graph(s) horizontal axes?

Appendix Six

Expected Output—Applied Graphing Assignment

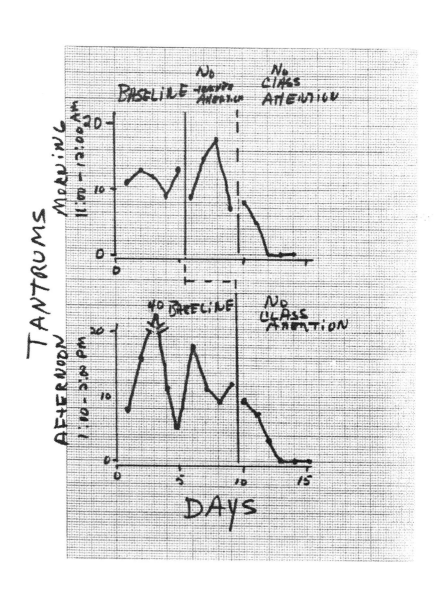

APPENDIX SEVEN

POST-TUTORIAL QUESTIONNAIRE

1 What course are you in?
   (a) 3214   (b) 3228   (c) 6211   (d) 6215

2 Which method of tutorial did you experience?
   (a) Programmed   (b) Scrolling Text

Strongly Agree	Agree	Neutral	Disagree	Strongly Disagree
a	b	c	d	e

3 I feel very much at ease in using a computer.

   ◇   ◇   ◇   ◇   ◇

4 This method of learning contributed to my understanding of the material in this lesson.

   ◇   ◇   ◇   ◇   ◇

5 I usually had uninterrupted time in which to complete the tutorials for this segment of the class.

   ◇   ◇   ◇   ◇   ◇

6 I am a fast reader, comprehending and retaining what I read.

   ◇   ◇   ◇   ◇   ◇

7 I have participated in Distance Learning where the assignments were done and turned in online.

◇   ◇   ◇   ◇   ◇

8 I would like to take other classes using the teaching technique I experience with this graphing tutorial.

◇   ◇   ◇   ◇   ◇

9 I had a quiet, comfortable location to log in and complete the tutorials for this segment of the class.

◇   ◇   ◇   ◇   ◇

10 I usually remember what I have read, and can repeat it to another, in my own words.

◇   ◇   ◇   ◇   ◇

11 I am very comfortable with my skills at using a computer and the internet.

◇   ◇   ◇   ◇   ◇

12 The way I completed these lessons is a great way to take a class.

◇   ◇   ◇   ◇   ◇

13 While doing these online tutorials, I completed the lessons without interruption.

◇   ◇   ◇   ◇   ◇

14 I took notes while completing the online lessons for this graphing segment of the class.

◇   ◇   ◇   ◇   ◇

15 I viewed the 11 lessons in sequence from start to end, following instructions at the end of the tutorial.

◇   ◇   ◇   ◇   ◇

APPENDIX EIGHT

FOLLOW-UP ONLINE QUESTIONNAIRE

Number of questions: 6

Question 1

Did you simply complete the tutorials you were assigned only, with no further studying?

a. Yes
b. No

Save answer

Question 2

How much more confident do you feel now about your ability to produce a graph from data in a behavioral study than you did before this segment of the class?

a. Very confident
b. Confident
c. Somewhat confident
d. Not too confident
e. Not confident at all.

Save answer

Question 3

Did you work with a friend / partner?

  a. Yes
  b. No

`Save answer`

Question 4

There were two forms of tutorials. One was programmed instruction with blanks to fill in. The other was the programmed instruction frames, but the answers were already filled in and italicized. (You may not have known about this.) Which one did you experience?

  a. Programmed instruction condition
  b. Read text condition
  c. found a way to study both

`Save answer`

Question 5

Given the choice, which of the following forms of instruction would you prefer when learning new materials?

  a. On-line programmed Instruction
  b. On-line Web Page Text & Graphics
  c. Classroom Lecture
  d. Group Study
  e. One-on-one tutoring

`Save answer`

Question 6

If you did any additional study for the graphing lessons beyond the on-line tutorials provided to you, what did you do? Please describe your additional study in the block below. (For example–additional book research, notes, printed out the tutorial pages and studied them, group study, practice graph drawing, etc.)

{Please type your answer here.}

Equation [Create new equation ▾] [Equation editor]

[Save answer]

[Finish] [Help]

APPENDIX NINE

NARRATIVE COMMENTS—QUESTION #6

Printed out some of the pages and read them over a couple of times.

I took a few notes on some of the terms that I was having repeated problems with during the tutorials. I reviewed the notes briefly before the exam.

I wrote my own notes then copied the study questions given to me then studied those.

I printed all of the questions from the programmed tutorials and reviewed them before the exam.

I took notes as I went along the tutorials.

I took notes and studied them.

I printed out the text version I was assigned and highlighted what I felt was important. I read it over a few times.

While I read the tutorials, I took notes on a separate sheet of paper.

I printed the tutorial out so that I could take my time and study the information.

I did the programmed tutorials more than once.

I printed select pages of the tutorial and reviewed them, reviewed tutorials several times.

Printed out some of the tutorials and reviewed them before taking the test.

I printed some tutorial pages out and tried to study them.

Looked and read briefly chapter 4 graphing data.

I print out the text tutorial and study them. I went through and highlighted and took notes on what I thought was the important part of the tutorial. I would look over the material for an hour and a half each day.

The only type of studying I did besides the tutorials was a little bit of group discussion. My partner and I tried to help each other understand what was actually going on.

I printed out the tutorials and studied them.

I made some notes while working through the tutorials, and reviewed those right before the tests.

I did do a little bit of extra studying. I read a few pages out of the text book and I even wrote down a few notes.

I printed out the last three tutorials because I thought of them to be more of a review of all the tutorials.

I printed the pages, and read them but just once because we did not had enough time, It was a lot of material in just one week.

Took some notes on the read text condition and reviewed them.

Printed out tutorial pages and studied them.

I printed the tutorial pages and studied them.

I printed out the tutorials and studied them, mainly the graphs.

I printed out the information and studied them. I paid particular attention to the words in italic print.

I did print off the tutorials and study them.

I printed out tutorial questions that I had trouble answering and studied them in addition to doing the tutorials.

I did take some time to view other graphs in certain books and I also recalled working on graphs in a couple of math classes I had taken and what was involved in the construction of them.

I printed out the tutorial pages and studied them.

I took some notes from the online program instruction.

I reviewed the questions twice before the exam by rereading most of the frames. I also printed some of the important questions I felt were necessary for studying.

Reviewed a small number of notes that I had made while doing the tutorials.

Online tutorials were followed and printed out for study. No research outside the online tutorial was done.

I printed out my tutorials and studied them at home.

While I was doing the tutorials I tried to write down the information that seemed to be pertinent. Before the test I reviewed the notes.

I wasn't able to print out the tutorials so I took notes from them directly.

I wrote a few notes.

I took notes of concepts I thought I might need to look over before the test while working through the programmed instruction.

I printed out the tutorials and studied them.

I printed out the tutorial pages and read them a few times.

I took notes for every tutorial I worked through.

I studied the graphs in chapters 4 & 5 in the textbook.

I decided to read chapter 4 in the Alberto book to try to understand what the graphing portion of the test was designed suppose to show us as educators.

Printed out the tutorial pages as there was way too much information to read and absorb.

I read chapter 4 and completed the study questions I printed the tutorial pages and highlighted them as I read them. I made notes as I read the printed pages. Then I reviewed my highlights and notes again before I went in to take the quiz.

Looked over Chapter 4 in the Alberto book.

I printed out the text pages and read them about 4 times and high-lighted what I felt was the most important material. Then after reading the material thoroughly for the 4th time I only looked back at what I highlighted. I also tried to study a little before I actually went in and took the quiz.

I read chapter 4 in our Alberto book plus I printed out the information from the tutorial and read it, twice. I memorized parts of the graph, etc., that apparently weren't important. It would have been helpful to know what you wanted from us.

I just reread the tutorial over and over again.

I did a little bit of practice graph drawing.

I performed the tutorial and then just looked over Chapter 4 on graphing in Alberto.

Printed out and made study cards.

I did print out the text I was assigned to read to further study it.

Printed out the text tutorial and reviewed material.

I practiced graphing by graphing other information found online.

Appendix Ten

Sample PERL Code for PI Treatment

```perl
#!/usr/local/bin/perl
use CGI;
use warnings;
$query = new CGI;

####################################################
###############################
###   MODIFY HERE     #########
# do not use quotes otherwise you must escape them
ie. \"

### Critical Changes ######
#0. The name of the table in the database
containing the output for this tutorial set
#    Leave blank quotes for outfiles
my $table = '';

#1. The title that will appear in the window title
bar (up top)
my $html_title = 'Graphing in Applied Behavior
Analysis';

#2. this is the title and brief description of what
the set is about (on the MAIN MENU) You can use
vaild html but be careful with quotes, escape them.
my $page_header =
qq(
<table cellpadding="2" cellspacing="2" border="0"
style="text-align: center; margin-left: auto;
margin-right: auto; width: 90%;">
<tbody>

<tr>
<td style;"center-align: top;"
<h2><strong><font color="#FF0000"
size="20">Graphing in Applied Behavior
Analysis<p><font size="6"></h2>
</table>
```

```
<hr>
<strong>The following instructional sets should be
accomplished in serial order:</strong>
<hr>
);

#3. tutorial list setup. this is the radio button list
along with the displayed description
#  file name followed by => then followed by the
single-quoted dscription; finally a comma (except
for the last entry
my %tutorial_setup =
(
'graphingset1_textfile.txt' => 'Graphing in Applied
Behavior Analysis Set 1',
'graphingset2_textfile.txt' => 'Graphing in Applied
Behavior Analysis Set 2',
'graphingset3_textfile.txt' => 'Graphing in Applied
Behavior Analysis Set 3',
'graphingset4_textfile.txt' => 'Graphing in Applied
Behavior Analysis Set 4',
'graphingset5_textfile.txt' => 'Graphing in Applied
Behavior Analysis Set 5',
'graphingset6_textfile.txt' => 'Graphing in Applied
Behavior Analysis Set 6',
'graphingset7_textfile.txt' => 'Graphing in Applied
Behavior Analysis Set 7',
'graphingset8_textfile.txt' => 'Graphing in Applied
Behavior Analysis Set 8',
'graphingset9_textfile.txt' => 'Graphing in Applied
Behavior Analysis Set 9',
'graphingset10_textfile.txt' => 'Graphing in Applied
Behavior Analysis Set 10',
'graphingset11_textfile.txt' => 'Graphing in Applied
Behavior Analysis Set 11'

);

#4. this is a list of the file names This is done so
that the radio buttons are displayed in the correct
order.
my @tutorial_files =
```

```
(
  'graphingset1_textfile.txt',
  'graphingset2_textfile.txt',
  'graphingset3_textfile.txt',
  'graphingset4_textfile.txt',
  'graphingset5_textfile.txt',
  'graphingset6_textfile.txt',
  'graphingset7_textfile.txt',
  'graphingset8_textfile.txt',
  'graphingset9_textfile.txt',
  'graphingset10_textfile.txt',
  'graphingset11_textfile.txt',
);

#5. the tutorial that will be checked by default
Must the same as one of the filenames above or none
will be checked by default.
my $default_tutorial = 'xx';

##### Optional Changes #######

#percent required to continue with tutorials
my $percentstartover = 20;

####### END MODIFICATIONS #################
#######################################################
############################

my $DSN = 'bostowtables';

$path_info = $query->path_info;
$fulladdress = $query->url();
$base_dir = $query->url();
$relative = $query->url(-relative=>1);
$base_dir =~ s/\/$relative//;
my $absol= $query->url(-absolute=>1);
$absol =~ s/\/$relative//;
$absol =~ s/\///\\/g;
my $absolute_dir =
'e:\inetpub\wwwroot\coedu'.$absol;

chdir $absolute_dir;
if ($path_info)
{
  $path_info =~ s/\///;
  my ($key, $val) = split(/=/,$path_info);
```

```
   if (defined($val) )
   {       &$val;         }
   else
   {   &doMainMenu;    }
}
else
{   &doMainMenu;  }

sub doMain
{
&GetParameters;

&GetNumberOfQuestions;

print $query->header(-type=>'text/html', -
expires=>'now');
print $query->start_html(-title=>"PI PLAYER
$html_title",-author=>'Kale Kritch mod by Darrel
Davis',-BGCOLOR=>'#FFFFFF');

print qq(

<script language="Javascript">
<!--
javascript:window.history.forward(1);
//-->
</script>
);
if ($UserAnswer eq "FirstVisit") {

    if ($QuestionNumber > $NumberOfQuestions) {
    $UserAnswer = "FINALSCORE";
    $Percent = $AnsweredCorrectly /
$NumberOfAttempts * 100;
    $Percent = substr($Percent, 0, 4);
    print "<BR>\n";
    print "<p align=\"center\"><b>You have reached
the end of this program.</b></p>\n";
    print "<div align=\"center\">\n";
    print "<center>\n";
    print "<table border=\"2\" width=\"66%\">\n";
    print   "<tr>\n";
    print       "<td width=\"80\%\">Number of frames
in this tutorial</td>\n";
    print       "<td
```

```
width=\"20\%\">$NumberOfQuestions</td>\n";
    print    "</tr>\n";
    print    "<tr>\n";
    print      "<td width=\"80\%\">Number of frames
you attempted</td>\n";
    print       "<td
width=\"20\%\">$NumberOfAttempts</td>\n";
    print    "</tr>\n";
    print    "<tr>\n";
    print      "<td width=\"80\%\">Number of
attempted frames you answered correctly</td>\n";
    print       "<td
width=\"20\%\">$AnsweredCorrectly</td>\n";
    print    "</tr>\n";
    print    "<tr>\n";
    print      "<td width=\"80\%\">Percent correct
score of attempted frames</td>\n";
    print       "<td
width=\"20\%\">$Percent\%</td>\n";
    print    "</tr>\n";
    print  "</table>\n";
    print  "</center>\n";
    print "</div>\n";
    print "<BR>\n";
    print "<CENTER><strong><a
href=\"$MainMenuAddress\"> Click here to return to
    the Main Menu</a></strong></CENTER><BR>\n";

    &WriteOutFile;
    exit;
    }
  $TryNumber = 1;
  &ShowFrame;
  &AskForResponse;
  &OutputVariables;
} else {
  &EvaluateResponse;
}
  print $query->end_html;
}


sub doMainMenu
```

```
{
      print $query->header(-type=>'text/html',
-expires=>'now');
      print $query->start_html(-title=>$html_title,-
author=>'Kale Kritch mod by Darrel Davis',-
BGCOLOR=>'#66CCFF');
#print "<br>-------------absol= $absolute_dir-----

-------------<br>referer=$origin <br>fulladdress=

$fulladdress <br> path_info=

$path_info <br> base_dir= $base_dir <br>full=

",$query- >url(),"<br>relative= ",$query->url(-

relative=>1),"<br>absolute=",$query->url(-

absolute=>1),"<br>with path=

",$query->url(-path_info=>1),"<br>with path and
query=",$query->url(-path_info=>1,-
query=>1),"<br>net location = ",$query->url(-base
=> 1),"<br>------------------<br>";

      print qq(

<script language="JavaScript">
<!--

function verify(userEntry) {
      aCharExists=0
      entry=userEntry
      if (entry) {
          if (entry.charAt(0) != "") {
          aCharExists=1
              }
      }
      if (!aCharExists) {
          window.alert("Please enter your full
name.")

document.PIMenu_Form.StudentName.focus()
      }
}
//-->
</script>
```

```
<form name="PIMenu_Form" method="post"
action="$fulladdress/destination=doMain">
$page_header
<p align="center"><font color="#FF0000" size="5">
Main Menu</font></p>
<P>Follow the <strong>4 Steps</strong> below to
experience the on-line tutorials.</P>

<input type="hidden" name="MainMenuAddress"
value="$fulladdress">
<input type="hidden" name="PercentStartOver"
value=$percentstartover>

<input type="hidden" name="UserAnswer"
value="FirstVisit">
<strong>Step 1 - Type your full name (e.g. Mary
Smith):</strong><br>
<input type="text" name="StudentName" size="30"
onBlur="verify(this.value)">
<p>
<strong>Step 2 - Select a tutorial by clicking once
in the radio button beside the
tutorial:</strong><br>
<h3><font color=green>Before selecting a tutorial,
scroll down and note the tutorials you have already
done.<br>
Make sure your records show all 11 tutorials as
completed, and be sure to type your name the same
way every time.
</font></h3>
);
print $query->radio_group(-
name=>'TutorialSelection', -
values=>\@tutorial_files, -
default=>$default_tutorial, -linebreak=>'true', -
labels=>\%tutorial_setup);

print qq(
<!-- <strong>Step 3 - Enter Frame Number (If you
are working through the tutorial for the first
time, leave as 1 If you are reviewing, enter the
frame number you wish to begin working
```

```
on):</strong><br>
--><input type="hidden" name="QuestionNumber"
size="4" value="1"></p>
<p>
<strong>Step 3- Click Begin Tutorial: </strong><br>
<input type="submit" value="Begin Tutorial"> </p>
</form>

<br><br>Completion List:<br>
<table border=1>
<tr><td>Name</td><td>Tutorial Completed</td></tr>
);
my @complist; my $compname; my $comptut;
open (COMPFILE, "completions.txt");
  while (<COMPFILE>)
  {   push @complist,$_  }
close (COMPFILE);
 @complist = sort {uc($a) cmp uc($b)} @complist;
foreach (@complist)
{
    ($compname, $comptut) = split('&&', $_);
    $compname=$compname.""; $comptut=$comptut."";
    print "<tr><td> $compname </td><td> $comptut
</td></tr>";

    print qq(</table>
<script>
document.PIMenu_Form.StudentName.focus()</script>
);
    print $query->end_html;
}

sub GetParameters
{
$MainMenuAddress = $query->param('MainMenuAddress');
$PercentStartOver = $query->param('PercentStartOver');
$UserAnswer = $query->param('UserAnswer');
$TutorialSelection = $query->
param('TutorialSelection');
$StudentName = $query->param('StudentName');
$RemoteAddress = $query->param('REMOTE_ADDR');
$BrowserType = $query->param('HTTP_USER_AGENT');
$QuestionNumber = $query->param('QuestionNumber');
```

```perl
$TryNumber = $query->param('TryNumber');
$NumberOfQuestions = $query-
>param('NumberOfQuestions');
$NumberOfAttempts = $query-
>param('NumberOfAttempts');
$AnsweredCorrectly = $query-
>param('AnsweredCorrectly');
$Tries = $query->param('Tries');
$OutFileName = $TutorialSelection;
$OutFileName =~ s/.txt/_Out.txt/;
}
sub GetNumberOfQuestions
{
$NumberOfQuestions = 0;
open (CAIFILE, "$TutorialSelection");
  while (<CAIFILE>)
  {
    if (index($_,'@begin',0) > -1)
    {
      $NumberOfQuestions++;
      }
    }
close (CAIFILE);
}

sub ShowFrame
{
print "<strong>Frame #: $QuestionNumber of
$NumberOfQuestions</strong><br>\n";
print "<strong>Try #: $TryNumber</strong><br>\n";
if ($NumberOfAttempts > 1) {
  $Percent = $AnsweredCorrectly / $NumberOfAttempts
* 100;
  $Percent = substr($Percent, 0, 4);
  print "<strong>Correct %:
$Percent</strong><br>\n";
}
if ($NumberOfAttempts > 4 and $Percent <
$PercentStartOver){
    UserAnswer = "STARTOVER";
    $Percent = $AnsweredCorrectly /
$NumberOfAttempts * 100;
    $Percent = substr($Percent, 0, 4);
```

```
    print "<BR>\n";
    print "<CENTER><strong><FONT
COLOR=\"#ff0000\">Your percent correct is less than
$PercentStartOver after at least 5
frames.</FONT></strong></CENTER><BR>\n";
    print "<CENTER><strong><FONT
COLOR=\"#ff0000\">You are required to exit this
tutorial and begin
again.</FONT></strong></CENTER><BR>\n";
    print "<CENTER><strong>Total number of possible
questions in this tutorial:
$NumberOfQuestions</strong></CENTER><BR>\n";
    print "<CENTER><strong>Total number of
questions you attempted:
$NumberOfAttempts</strong></CENTER><BR>\n";
    print "<CENTER><strong>Number of attempted
questions you answered correctly:
$AnsweredCorrectly</strong></CENTER><BR>\n";
    print "<CENTER><strong>Percent score of
attempted questions: $Percent\%</CENTER><BR>\n";
    print "<CENTER><strong><a
href=\"$MainMenuAddress\"> Click here to return to
the Main Menu</a></strong></CENTER><BR>\n";
    &WriteOutFile;
    exit;
}
print "<p>\n";
local ($Number);
$Number = 0;
open(CAIFILE,"$TutorialSelection");
  while (<CAIFILE>)  {
    if (index($_,'@begin',0) > -1)  {
    $Number++;
      if ($Number == $QuestionNumber) {
      $line = <CAIFILE>;
      print "<strong>\n";
        while (index($line,'@end',0) < 0)  {
        print "$line<br>\n";
        $line = <CAIFILE>;    }
        while (index($line,'@answer',0) < 0)  {
          $line = <CAIFILE>;    }
          $CorrectAnswer = substr($line,8);
```

```perl
            chomp($CorrectAnswer);
              $CorrectAnswer = lc($CorrectAnswer);
          while (index($line,'@tries',0) < 0)   {
            $line = <CAIFILE>;    }
            $Tries = substr($line,7);
            chomp($Tries);
          while (index($line,'@graphic',0) < 0)   {
            $line = <CAIFILE>;    }
            $Graphic = substr($line,9);

            chomp($Graphic);
          while (index($line,'@video',0) < 0)   {
            $line = <CAIFILE>;    }
            $Video = substr($line,7);
            chomp($Video);
        }
      }
    }
close(CAIFILE);
#local($index);
if ($Graphic ne "none") {
  print "<CENTER><IMG
SRC=\"..\/..\/graphics\/$Graphic\"></CENTER>\n"; }
if ($Video ne "none") {
  print "<p><a href=\"$Video\">Click here to view
the video</a></p>\n"; }
}

sub OutputVariables
{
print <<EOT;
<INPUT NAME=\"MainMenuAddress\" TYPE=\"HIDDEN\"
VALUE=\"$MainMenuAddress\">
<INPUT NAME=\"PercentStartOver\" TYPE=\"HIDDEN\"
VALUE=\"$PercentStartOver\">
<INPUT NAME=\"TutorialSelection\" TYPE=\"HIDDEN\"
VALUE=\"$TutorialSelection\">
<INPUT NAME=\"StudentName\" TYPE=\"HIDDEN\"
VALUE=\"$StudentName\">
<INPUT NAME=\"QuestionNumber\" TYPE=\"HIDDEN\"
VALUE=\"$QuestionNumber\">
<INPUT NAME=\"TryNumber\" TYPE=\"HIDDEN\"
```

```perl
VALUE=\"$TryNumber\">
<INPUT NAME=\"NumberOfQuestions\" TYPE=\"HIDDEN\"
VALUE=\"$NumberOfQuestions\">
<INPUT NAME=\"NumberOfAttempts\" TYPE=\"HIDDEN\"
VALUE=\"$NumberOfAttempts\">
<INPUT NAME=\"AnsweredCorrectly\" TYPE=\"HIDDEN\"
VALUE=\"$AnsweredCorrectly\">
<INPUT NAME=\"Tries\" TYPE=\"HIDDEN\"
VALUE=\"$Tries\">
</FORM>
EOT
}

sub AskForResponse
{
print <<EOT;
<script language="JavaScript">
</script>
<body
onLoad="document.AskForAnswer_Form.UserAnswer.focus
()">
<form method=post name="AskForAnswer_Form">
<strong>Type your answer here: </strong>

<INPUT NAME="UserAnswer" TYPE="text" ALIGN=left
SIZE="30" AUTOCOMPLETE="OFF">
EOT
#print "<p><strong>Total Possible Tries for this
Frame: $Tries</strong>\n";
}

sub EvaluateResponse
{
local ($Number);
$Number = 0;
# Look up what the correct answer should be here:
  open(CAIFILE,"$TutorialSelection");
  while (<CAIFILE>) {
          if (index($_,'@begin',0) > -1) {
                $Number++;
                if ($Number == $QuestionNumber) {
                    $line = <CAIFILE>;
                    while (index($line,'@end',0) <
```

```
0) {
                                    $line = <CAIFILE>;
                                    }
                        while
   (index($line,'@answer',0) < 0) {
                              $line = <CAIFILE>;
                              }
                        $CorrectAnswer =
substr($line,8);
                        chomp($CorrectAnswer);
                  }
            }
      }
   close(CAIFILE);
  if (lc($UserAnswer) eq lc($CorrectAnswer) and
$TryNumber <= $Tries) {
      $FeedBack = "CORRECT";
      $AnsweredCorrectly++;
      $NumberOfAttempts++;
      &WriteOutFile;
      &ShowFrame;
      print "<BR>\n";
      print "<CENTER><strong>Your answer <FONT
      COLOR=\"#0000ff\">$UserAnswer</FONT> is <FONT
COLOR=\"#008000\">$FeedBack!</FONT></strong></CENTER>
\n";
      print "<CENTER><strong>Press Enter or Click to
Continue.</strong></CENTER>\n";
      $QuestionNumber++;
      &ContinueButton;
      &OutputVariables;
  }
  if (lc($UserAnswer) ne lc($CorrectAnswer) and
$TryNumber < $Tries) {
      $FeedBack = "INCORRECT";
      &WriteOutFile;

      $TryNumber = $TryNumber + 1;
      &ShowFrame;
      &AskForResponse;
      print "<BR>\n";
      print "<CENTER><strong>Your answer <FONT
```

```
COLOR=\"#0000ff\">$UserAnswer</FONT> is <FONT
COLOR=\"#ff0000\">$FeedBack</FONT>.</strong></CENTER>
\n";
    print "<CENTER><strong>Please try
again.</strong></CENTER><BR>";
      &OutputVariables;
  }
  elsif (lc($UserAnswer) ne lc($CorrectAnswer) and
$TryNumber >= $Tries) {
    $NumberOfAttempts++;
    $FeedBack = "INCORRECT";
    &WriteOutFile;
    &ShowFrame;
    print "<BR>\n";
    print "<CENTER><strong>Your answer <FONT
COLOR=\"#0000ff\">$UserAnswer</FONT> is <FONT
COLOR=\"#ff0000\">$FeedBack</FONT>.</strong></CENTER>
\n";
    print "<CENTER><strong>The correct answer was
<FONT
COLOR=\"#0000ff\">$CorrectAnswer</FONT>.</strong>
</CENTER>\n";
    $QuestionNumber++;
    $TryNumber = 1;
    &ContinueButton;
    &OutputVariables;
  }
}
#end of EvaluateResponse

sub ContinueButton
{
print <<EOT;
<script language="JavaScript">
</script>
<body
onLoad="document.ContinueButton_Form.ContinueButton.
focus()">
<form method=post name="ContinueButton_Form">
<center><input name="ContinueButton" type=submit
value="Continue"></center>
<input name=\"UserAnswer\" type=\"hidden\"
```

```
value=\"FirstVisit\">
EOT
}

sub PrintScalars
{
print "TutorialSelection = $TutorialSelection<br>\n";
print "UserAnswer = $UserAnswer<br>\n";
print "StudentName = $StudentName<br>\n";
print "RemoteAddress = $RemoteAddress<br>\n";

print "BrowserType = $BrowserType<br>\n";
print "QuestionNumber = $QuestionNumber<br>\n";
print "TryNumber = $TryNumber<br>\n";
print "NumberOfQuestions = $NumberOfQuestions<br>\n";
print "NumberOfAttempts = $NumberOfAttempts<br>\n";
print "AnsweredCorrectly = $AnsweredCorrectly<br>\n";
print "CorrectAnswer = $CorrectAnswer<br>\n";
print "Graphic = $Graphic<br>\n";
print "Tries = $Tries<br>\n";
print "TutorialSelection = $TutorialSelection<br>\n";
print "OutFileName = $OutFileName<br>\n";
}
sub ExitButton
{
print "<HR WIDTH=100\% ALIGN=center SIZE=2>\n";
print "<LEFT><INPUT NAME=\"Exit\" TYPE=\"SUBMIT\"
ALIGN=absmiddle\n";
print "VALUE=\"Exit Program\"></LEFT>";
}

sub WriteOutFile
{
$Percent = substr($Percent, 0, 4);
$TimeStamp = localtime (time);
open(OUTFILE,">>$OutFileName") or dienice("Can't open
outfile.txt for writing: $!");
# This locks the file so no other CGI can write to it
at the same time
# flock(OUTFILE,2);
# Reset the file pointer to the end of the file, in
case someone wrote while we waited for lock
seek(OUTFILE,0,2);
```

```perl
print OUTFILE "$StudentName,";
print OUTFILE "$TutorialSelection,";
print OUTFILE "$QuestionNumber,";
print OUTFILE "$TryNumber,";
print OUTFILE "$CorrectAnswer,";
print OUTFILE "$UserAnswer,";
print OUTFILE "$FeedBack,";
print OUTFILE "$NumberOfQuestions,";
print OUTFILE "$NumberOfAttempts,";
print OUTFILE "$AnsweredCorrectly,";
print OUTFILE "$Percent,";
print OUTFILE "$TimeStamp\n";
close(OUTFILE);

if ($UserAnswer eq "FINALSCORE")
{
my $tutsel=$TutorialSelection;
$tutsel =~ s/graphingset//;

$tutsel =~ s/_textfile.txt//;
open(CMPFILE,">>completions.txt") or dienice("Can't
open completions_alb.txt for writing: $!");
print CMPFILE "$StudentName&&$tutsel\n";
close(CMPFILE);
}

}

# The dienice subroutine, for handling errors
sub dienice
{
my($errmsg) = @_;
print "<h2>Error</h2>\n";
print "$errmsg<p>\n";
print "</body></html>\n";
exit;
}
```

APPENDIX ELEVEN

SAMPLE HTML FOR CUED-TEXT TREATMENT

```
<?xml version="1.0" encoding="utf-8"?>
<!DOCTYPE html
    PUBLIC "-//W3C//DTD XHTML Basic 1.0//EN"
    "http://www.w3.org/TR/xhtml-basic/xhtml-
basic10.dtd">
<html xmlns="http://www.w3.org/1999/xhtml"
lang="en-US"><head><title>PI PLAYER Graphing in
Applied Behavior Analysis</title>
<link rev="made"
href="mailto:Kale%20Kritch%20mod%20by%20Darrel%20Davis" />
</head><body bgcolor="#FFFFFF">
<script language="Javascript">
<!--
javascript:window.history.forward(1);
//-->
</script>
<h3><u><strong><font color=green>Click the button at
the end of the text when you have completed the
reading</font></strong></u></h3><div class=Section1>
  <p><strong>When more than <span
class=GramE><i>three</i>  data</span> paths
    must be included on the same graph, other methods
of display can be incorporated.
    <u1:p></u1:p></strong></p>
</div>
<strong><br
clear=all style='page-break-before:auto;'>
</strong>
<div class=Section2 style="width: 766; height: 166">
  <p> <img width=221 height=124
src="../../Graphics/figure27.gif" align="right"
hspace="20" vspace="20" align=left hspace=12
v:shapes="_x0000_s1026"><strong>The bar graph, or
```

```
histogram, is a </strong>  <strong>simple
    and versatile format for graphically summarizing
behavioral data. Like the
line graph, the bar graph is based on the Cartesian
plane and shares most
    of the line graph's features with one primary
difference: the bar graph <i>does
    not have</i> distinct data points representing
successive response measures
    through time. </strong></p>
</div>
<strong><br
clear=all style='page-break-before:auto;'>
</strong>
<div class=Section3> </div>
<strong><br
clear=all style='page-break-before:auto;'>
</strong>
<div class=Section4 style="width: 770; height: 295">
  <p><strong><span style='font-weight:normal'>
    <img width=308 height=253
src="../../Graphics/figure28.gif" align="right"
hspace="20" vspace="20"
v:shapes="_x0000_i1027"></span>
  <p> </p>  <p> </p>Line graphs with the
data points connected imply that the same variable
    is being measured across time-say, number of
fights on the playground. 
    Bar graphs serve two major functions in the
display of data. First, a bar
    graph <span class=GramE>is</span> used when the
sets of data to be compared
    <i>are not</i> related to one another by a common
underlying dimension by
    which the horizontal axis can be scaled. The
figure here is an example of
    a bar graph displaying and comparing such discrete
data. <span style='font-weight:normal'>
     </span> </strong></p>
</div>
<strong><br
clear=all style='page-break-before:auto;'>
```

```
</strong>
<div class=Section5> </div>
<strong><br
clear=all style='page-break-before:auto;'>
</strong>
<div class=Section6 style="width: 770; height: 375">
  <p><strong><span style='font-weight:normal'> <img
width=225 height=333
src="../../Graphics/figure29.gif" align="right"
hspace="20" vspace="20"
v:shapes="_x0000_i1028"></span>
  <p> </p>  <p> </p>  <p> </p>
<p> </p>The second most common use of the BAR
graph is to give a visual summary
    of the performance of a subject or group of
subjects during the different
    <i>conditions </i>of an experiment. </strong></p>
  <p><strong><span style='font-weight:normal'>
 </span>  </strong></p>
</div>
<strong><br
clear=all style='page-break-before:auto;'>
</strong>
<div class=Section7 style="width: 768; height: 375">
  <p><strong><span style='font-weight:normal'>
    <img width=225 height=333
src="../../Graphics/figure30.gif" align="right"
hspace="20" vspace="20"
v:shapes="_x0000_i1029"></span>
  <p> </p>  <p> </p>  <p> </p>
<p> </p>This figure shows two <i>bar</i> graphs
(light and dark) that summarize
    the percentage of male and female juvenile
offenders involved in criminal
    offenses before, during, and after treatment in a
teaching family home.</strong><strong><span
style='font-weight:normal'>  </span> 
</strong></p>
</div>
<strong><br
clear=all style='page-break-before:auto;'>
</strong>
<div class=Section8> </div>
<strong><br
```

```
clear=all style='page-break-before:auto;'>
</strong>
<div class=Section9 style="width: 771; height: 333">
  <p><strong><span
style='font-weight:normal'> <img width=197 height=291
src="../../Graphics/figure31.gif" align="right"
hspace="20" vspace="20"
v:shapes="_x0000_i1030"></span>
  <p> </p>   <p> </p>   <p> </p>
<p> </p>The <span class=GramE><i>bar
</i> graph</span> also permits
    comparison (upper and lower) of the subjects'
incidence of criminal involvement
    with that of similar youths who received treatment
in other group homes.</strong><strong><span
style='font-weight:normal'>  </span> 
</strong></p>
</div>
<strong><br
clear=all style='page-break-before:auto;'>
</strong>
<div class=Section10>
  <p><strong>Although bar graphs can also be used to
display range or trend, they
    are typically used to present a measure of central
tendency, such as the <i>mean</i>
    or median score for each condition.
<ul:p></ul:p></strong></p>
  <p><strong>A bar graph <i>sacrifices</i>
presentation of the variability and
    trends in behavior (which are apparent in a line
graph) in exchange for the
    efficiency of summarizing and comparing large
amounts of data in a simple,
    easy-to-interpret format.
<ul:p></ul:p></strong></p>
  <p><strong>Bar graphs can take a wide variety of
forms to allow a quick and
    easy comparison of performance across subjects or
conditions. However, bar
    graphs should be viewed with the understanding
that they may mask important
```

```
<span
class=GramE><i>variability</i>  in</span> the
data.<ul:p> </ul:p></strong></p>
</div>
<strong><br
clear=all style='page-break-before:auto;'>
</strong>
<div class=Section11 style="width: 776; height: 195">
  <p><strong><span style='font-weight:normal'> <img
width=231 height=153
src="../../Graphics/figure32.gif" align="right"
hspace="20" vspace="20"
v:shapes="_x0000_i1031"></span>
  <p> </p>  <p> </p>A cumulative graph is
one that goes only <i>up</i> as responses (data)
    are accumulated. <span style='font-weight:normal'>
 </span> </strong></p>
</div>
<otrong><br
clear=all style='page-break-before:auto;'>
</strong>

<div class=Section12>
  <p><strong>The CUMULATIVE record (or graph) was
developed by B. F. Skinner as
    the primary means of <i>data</i> collection and
analysis in laboratory research
    in the experimental analysis of behavior.
<ul:p></ul:p></strong></p>
</div>
<strong><br
clear=all style='page-break-before:auto;'>
</strong>
<div class=Section13 style="width: 781; height: 210">
  <p><strong><span
style='font-weight:normal'> <img width=236 height=168
src="../../Graphics/figure33.gif" align="right"
hspace="20" vspace="20"
v:shapes="_x0000_i1032"></span>
  <p> </p>  <p> </p>Skinner's device, called
the <span class=GramE><i>cumulative</i> 
recorder</span>, enables an experimental subject to
```

```
actually draw its own
    graph as it responds.</strong><strong><span
style='font-weight:normal'>  </span>
</strong></p>
</div>
<strong><br
clear=all style='page-break-before:auto;'>
</strong>
<div class=Section14> </div>
<strong><br
clear=all style='page-break-before:auto;'>
</strong>
<div class=Section15 style="width: 780; height: 285">
  <p><strong> <img width=264 height=211
src="../../Graphics/figure34.gif" align="right"
hspace="20" vspace="20" v:shapes="_x0000_i1033">In a
book cataloging 6 years of experimental research on
schedules
    of reinforcement, <span
class=SpellE>Ferster</span> and Skinner (1957)
described
    cumulative graphs in the following manner: 
&quot;A graph showing the
    number of responses on the ordinate against time
on the abscissa has proved
    to be the most convenient representation of the
behavior observed in this
    research. Fortunately, such a
&quot;cumulative&quot; record may be made directly
    at the time of the experiment. The record is raw
data, but it also permits
    a <i>direct inspection</i> of rate and changes in
rate not possible when the
    behavior is observed directly. Each time the bird
responds<span class=GramE>,</span>
    the pen moves one step across the
paper.&quot;  </strong></p>
</div>
<strong><br
clear=all style='page-break-before:auto;'>
</strong>
<div class=Section16> </div>
```

```
<strong><br
clear=all style='page-break-before:auto;'>
</strong>
<div class=Section17 style="width: 778; height: 210">
  <p><strong><span style='font-weight:normal'> <img
width=236 height=168
src="../../Graphics/figure35.gif" align="right"
hspace="20" vspace="20"
v:shapes="_x0000_i1034"></span>
  <p> </p>   <p> </p>At the same time, the
paper feeds continuously. If the bird does
    not respond at all, a <i>horizontal</i> line is
drawn in the direction of
    the paper feed.</strong><strong><span
style='font-weight:normal'>  </span> 
</strong></p>
</div>
<strong><br
clear=all style='page-break-before:auto;'>
</strong>
<div class=Section18 style="width: 779; height: 210">
  <p><strong><span
style='font-weight:normal'> <img width=236 height=168
src="../../Graphics/figure36.gif" align="right"
hspace="20" vspace="20"
v:shapes="_x0000_i1035"></span>   <p> </p>
<p> </p>The faster the person responds, the
<i>steeper</i> the line.</strong><strong><span
style='font-weight:normal'>  </span> 
</strong></p>
</div>
<strong><br
clear=all style='page-break-before:auto;'>
</strong>
<div class=Section19>
  <p><strong>When cumulative records are plotted by
hand, which is most often
    the case in applied behavior analysis, the number
of responses recorded during
    each observation period is added (thus the term
cumulative) to the <i>total</i>
    number of responses recorded during all previous
```

```
observation periods.
<ul:p></ul:p></strong></p>
  <p><strong>In a <i>cumulative</i> record, the Y-axis
value of any data point
     represents the total number of responses recorded
since the beginning of data
     collection. <ul:p></ul:p></strong></p>
</div>
<strong><br
clear=all style='page-break-before:auto;'>
</strong>
<div class=Section20 style="width: 779; height: 213">
  <p><strong> <img width=264 height=171
src="../../Graphics/figure37.gif" align="right"
hspace="20" vspace="20" v:shapes="_x0000_i1036">
<p> </p>In a cumulative record, the Y-axis value
of any data point represents
     the total number of responses recorded since the
beginning of data collection.
     The exception occurs when the total number of
responses has exceeded the upper
     limit of the Y-axis scale, in which case
cumulative curves <i>reset
</i>to yhe 0 value of the Y-axis and begin their
ascent again.  </strong></p>
</div>
<strong><br
clear=all style='page-break-before:auto;'>
</strong>
<div class=Section21>
  <p><strong>Cumulative records are almost always used
with frequency data, although
     other dimensions of behavior such as duration and
latency can be displayed
     <i>cumulatively</i>.<ul:p> </ul:p></strong></p>
</div>
<strong><br
clear=all style='page-break-before:auto;'>
</strong>
<div class=Section22 style="width: 777; height: 342">
  <p><strong> <img width=264 height=242
src="../../Graphics/figure38.gif" align="right"
```

hspace="20" vspace="20" v:shapes="_x0000_i1037">This
figure is an example of a <span
class=GramE><i>cumulative</i>
   record</span> from the applied behavior analysis
literature. It shows the
   number of spelling words mastered by a mentally
retarded man <span class=GramE>under</span>
   three conditions. </strong></p>
  <p><strong>The graph at the right shows that Subject
3 mastered a total of 1
   word during the 12 sessions of baseline (social
praise for correct spelling
   responses and rewriting incorrectly spelled words
three times), a total of
   22 words under the <span
class=SpellE><i>interspersal</i></span>
condition
   (baseline procedures plus the presentation of a
previously learned word after
   each unknown word), and a total of 11 words under
the high density reinforcement
   condition (baseline procedures plus social praise
given after each trial for
   task-related behaviors such as paying attention
and writing neatly). </strong></p>
</div>
<strong><br
clear=all style='page-break-before:auto;'>
</strong>
<div class=Section23>
  <p><strong><i>Rate</i> is the frequency of responses
emitted per unit of time,
   usually reported as responses per minute in
applied behavior analysis.<ul:p>
   </ul:p></strong></p>
  <p><strong>An "overall" response rate is
the <i>average</i> rate of
   response over a given time period, such as during
a specific session, phase,

   or condition of an experiment.
<ul:p></ul:p></strong></p>

```
<p><strong>Overall rates are calculated by dividing
the total number of responses
    recorded during the period by the number of
observation periods-- indicated
        on the <i>horizontal</i> axis.<ul:p>
</ul:p></strong></p>
    <p><strong>In addition to the <i>total</i> number of
responses recorded at any
        given point in time, cumulative records show the
overall and &quot;local&quot;
            response rates.<ul:p> </ul:p></strong></p>
</div>
<strong><br
clear=all style='page-break-before:auto;'>
</strong>
<div class=Section24 style="width: 773; height: 180">
   <p><strong> <img width=264 height=138
src="../../Graphics/figure40.gif" align="right"
hspace="20" vspace="20" v:shapes="_x0000_i1038">
<p> </p>   <p> </p>In the figure
   at the right, the <i>local</i> rate at the point of
the arrow
        is very high.  </strong></p>
</div>
<strong><br
clear=all style='page-break-before:auto;'>
</strong>
<div class=Section25> </div>
<strong><br
clear=all style='page-break-before:auto;'>
</strong>
<div class=Section26 style="width: 770; height: 285">
   <p><strong> <img width=264 height=243
src="../../Graphics/figure42.gif" align="right"
hspace="20" vspace="20" v:shapes="_x0000_i1039">
<p> </p>In this figure, the <i>overall</i>
response rates of words mastered
        per session are .46 for the <span
class=SpellE><span
class=GramE>interspersal</span></span><span
class=GramE>  and</span> .23 for high-density
reinforcement conditions.  </strong></p>
```

    `<p><strong> (Technically, data points do not represent true rates of response`
    `since the number of words spelled correctly was measured and not the rate,`
    `or speed, at which they were spelled. However, the <i>slope</i> of each data`
    `path does represent the different &quot;rates&quot; of mastering the spelling`
    `words in each session within the context of a total of 10 new words presented`
    `each day.)    </strong></p>`
`</div>`
`<strong><br`
`clear=all style='page-break-before:auto;'>`
`</strong>`
`<div class=Section27>`
  `<p><strong>On a cumulative graph, response rates are compared with one another`
    `by comparing the slope of each data path- the steeper the slope, the <span`
`class=GramE><i>higher  </i>the</span> response rate. <ul:p></ul:p></strong></p>`
  `<p><strong>On a cumulative graph, response rates are compared with one another`
    `by comparing the <i>slope</i> of each data path. <ul:p></ul:p></strong></p>`
`</div>`
`<strong><br`
`clear=all style='page-break-before:always;'>`
`</strong>`
`<div class=Section28 style="width: 772; height: 285">`
  `<p><strong> <img width=264 height=243`
`src="../../Graphics/figure43.gif" align="right" hspace="20" vspace="20" v:shapes="_x0000_i1040">`
`<p> </p> <p> </p> To produce a visual representation of an overall rate on a cumulative`
    `graph, the first and last data points of a given series of observations should`
    `be connected with a straight line. A straight line connecting Points a and`
    `c in this figure represents Subject 3's overall rate of mastering spelling`

```
    words during the<i> high density</i>
condition.  </strong></p>
</div>
<strong><br
clear=all style='page-break-before:auto;'>
</strong>
<div class=Section29> </div>
<SCRIPT LANGUAGE=JavaScript>
</SCRIPT>
<form method=post name="AskForAnswer_Form">
<br><br><center>
<INPUT NAME="UserAnswer" value = "Completed"
TYPE="submit" AUTOCOMPLETE="OFF"></center>
<INPUT NAME="MainMenuAddress" TYPE="HIDDEN"
VALUE="http://www.coedu.usf.edu/bostow/rcanton/text/
textplayer.pl">
<INPUT NAME="PercentStartOver" TYPE="HIDDEN"
VALUE="20">
<INPUT NAME="TutorialSelection" TYPE="HIDDEN"
VALUE="textset5_textfile.txt">
<INPUT NAME="StudentName" TYPE="HIDDEN" VALUE="tewst">
<INPUT NAME="QuestionNumber" TYPE="HIDDEN" VALUE="1">
<INPUT NAME="TryNumber" TYPE="HIDDEN" VALUE="1">
<INPUT NAME="NumberOfQuestions" TYPE="HIDDEN" VALUE="1">
<INPUT NAME="NumberOfAttempts" TYPE="HIDDEN" VALUE="1">
<INPUT NAME="AnsweredCorrectly" TYPE="HIDDEN" VALUE="1">
<INPUT NAME="Tries" TYPE="HIDDEN" VALUE="1">
</FORM>
</body></html>
```

APPENDIX TWELVE

CREATING COMPUTER PROGRAMMED INSTRUCTION

About Programmed Instruction (API) Sets
These programs introduce learners to the basic concepts of programmed instruction. Following are a list of the programs sets and the concepts that they teach.

Set 1: frames, technology, programmed instruction, initial & terminal behavior.

Set 2: observable behavior, probability, reinforcer, immediate reinforcement, emit.

Set 3: discriminative stimulus, SD, S^, occasion, discrimination.

Set 4: prompts, supplementary stimulation, fading.

Set 5: formal and thematic prompts, fading.

Set 6: control of observing behavior, blanks, formal prompts.

Set 7: discrimination training, stimulus control, fading.

Set 8: discrimination training, teach new concepts, stimulus control, fading.

Set 9: defining concepts as behavior, examples and definitions, grammatical contexts.

Set 10: frequent reinforcement, 10 percent error rate, revising.

Set 11: change behavior, graphics, use information, control observing behavior.

Set 12: controlled changes in behavior, technology that controls.

Set 13: teaching machines, progress at own rate.

Set 14: educators create programs, problems with multiple choice frames, constructed response.

Set 15: even and uneven distributions, evaluation, revision, program effectiveness.

Set 16: review of previous concepts.

Set 17: word erasing, control of observing behavior, location of blanks.

Set 18: progression, wasteful frames, tally of responses, sequencing, programmer is first student of program.

Set 19: contingency of reinforcement.

Preparing Automated Instruction (PAI) Sets

Set 1:   frame, learning, observable behavior, change, immediate reinforcement, probability, strengthening, contingency of reinforcement.

Set 2:   contiguous pairing, contingency, consequence, supplemental stimulus, prompt, fading, echoic behavior.

Set 3:   echoic, intraverbal, contiguous, fading, overt responses, frequent responses.

Set 4:   tact, intraverbal, echoic response, world of things, environment, application, functional relations.

Set 5:   frame, easy at first, conditioning history, linear vs. branching.

Set 6:   priming, prompting, history of conditioning, thematic prompt.

Set 7:   fading, planning ahead, improperly constructed programs, why past programs failed, terminal behaviors, terminal objectives, contingency.

Set 8:   generalization, specification of terminal objectives, subordinate objectives, content expert, application of learning principles.

Set 9:   rule, tact, contiguous pairing, rule/example, discrimination training, developmental order, list rules.

Set 10: RULEG System for programmed instruction part 1.

Set 11: RULEG System for programmed instruction part 2.

Set 12: review of RULEG System, rule, compare, relationships, order, review frames, revised rule list, contiguous pairing.

Set 13: generalization, intraverbal connections, blank at end of frame, everything in frame is important, applying rule, inductive / deductive frames.

Set 14: small steps, examples as prompts, rules before examples, too few examples, rule first, order, review.

Set 15: short frames, many examples, blank at end, graphics not necessary, principles of learning and programming.

Set 16: authoring program, synonyms, key pairing, short frames, lecture frame, reviewing programs, examples, reintroduction of concepts in review frames, field test, formal prompt, prime.

Set 17: immediate reinforcement, terminal objectives, intraverbal, tact, pretest / posttest, limits of PI, review of steps to create a program.

Ruleg Frame Types

These tutorials teach about how to use a set of systematic templates for constructing various kinds of instructional frames.

Effective Characteristics of Instructional Programs

These programs teach those characteristics and features of effective instructional programs. Program titles and the concepts they teach are listed.

Set 1: Introduction: A rationale for the programs.

Set 2: Instructional Objectives: Instructional objectives, specification before instruction, stated in terms of observable, overt behavior, measuring program effectiveness.

Set 3: Learner Prerequisites: Inclusion of prerequisite statements, stated in terms of observable, overt behavior.

Set 4: Learner Control: Directions, arrangement of topics, time estimates, location indicators, easy access to segments, exiting.

Set 5: Motivation: Steps from simple to complex, degree of instructional steps, high rates of success, low error rates, reinforcement.

Set 6: Screen Design: Text-intensive materials, supplemental documents, justification, windows of scrolling text, electronic page turning.

Set 7: Graphics, Audio, and Animation: To what degree do they help learners accomplish objectives, entertainment and instruction, distractions, correctly responding.

Set 8: Lesson Design: Self-paced progression, frequency of evoking student responses, feedback, demonstrate mastery before progression, review, private tutors.

Set 9: Interaction: Require responses, frequent & observable responses, responses relating to objectives, selecting and constructing responses, multiple-choice alternatives, Critical-response Rule, prompts and cues, gradually withdrawn, private tutors.

Set 10: Individualized Programs: Self-pacing, appropriate behavior, frequent interaction, small steps, low error rate, relevant examples, immediate feedback.

APPENDIX THIRTEEN

TREATMENT ASSIGNMENT NOTIFICATION

Hello,

As you know from Dr. Bostow's message, we will be having lessons on "Graphing in Applied Behavior Analysis." Your link to the lessons for this section is:

http://www.coedu.usf.edu/bostow/rcanton/programmed

Go to this URL. Read and follow the instructions at the BLUE menu screen CAREFULLY.

The individual quiz times for these tutorials will be assigned by your course instructor. Complete all eleven tutorials before your assigned testing time. (Feb 2–7)

Thank you.

APPENDIX FOURTEEN

RELIABILITY CALCULATIONS TEMPLATES

(Applied Graphing Task-excerpt)

[online]

http://www.gifted.uconn.edu/siegle/research/Instrument%20Reliability %20and%20Validity/reliabilitycalculator2.xls

Cronbach's Alpha	0.848720447	Reliability Calculator	
Split-Half (odd-even) Correlation	0.808325024	created by Del Siegle (dsiegle@uconn.edu)	
Spearman-Brown Prophecy	0.894004135		
Mean for Test	13.84722222		
Standard Deviation for Test	4.924879362		
KR21	0.749649293	Questions	Participants
KR20	0.848720447	27	144

	Question 1	Question 2	Question 3	Question 4
Participant1	1	1	1	1
Participant2	1	1	0	0
Participant3	1	1	1	1
Participant4	1	1	1	1
Participant5	0	1	0	0
Participant6	1	1	0	0
Participant7	0	1	0	0
Participant8	1	1	0	0
Participant9	0	1	0	0
Participant10	1	1	0	0

(Continued)

	Question 1	Question 2	Question 3	Question 4
Participant11	1	1	0	0
Participant12	1	1	0	0
Participant13	1	1	1	1
Participant14	1	1	1	1
Participant15	1	1	0	0
Participant16	0	1	0	0
Participant17	1	1	0	0
Participant18	1	1	0	0
Participant19	0	1	0	0
Participant20	0	1	0	0
Participant21	1	0	0	0
Participant22	0	0	0	0
Participant23	0	0	0	0
Participant24	0	1	0	0

[online]
http://www.gifted.uconn.edu/siegle/research/Instrument%20Reliabilit
y%20and%20Validity/reliabilitycalculator2.xls

Cronbach's Alpha	0.873990452	**Reliability Calculator**
Split-Half (odd-even) Correlation	0.816034621	created by Del Siegle (dsiegle@uconn.edu)
Spearman-Brown Prophecy	0.89869941	
Mean for Test	20.08074534	
Standard Deviation for Test	8.608803204	
KR21	0.845461693	Questions Participants
KR20	0.873990452	54 161

	Question 1	Question 2	Question 3	Question 4
Participant1	0	1	1	0
Participant2	0	0	0	0
Participant3	0	1	0	0
Participant4	0	0	0	0
Participant5	0	0	0	0
Participant6	1	0	0	0
Participant7	1	1	1	0
Participant8	0	1	0	0
Participant9	0	1	1	0
Participant10	0	0	1	0
Participant11	0	0	0	0
Participant12	1	0	1	0
Participant13	1	0	0	0
Participant14	0	0	0	0
Participant15	0	1	0	0
Participant16	0	1	0	0
Participant17	0	0	0	0
Participant18	0	0	0	0
Participant19	0	1	1	0
Participant20	0	1	1	0
Participant21	0	1	1	0
Participant22	1	0	1	0
Participant23	1	0	0	0
Participant24	0	0	0	0

REFERENCES

Allen, B. S., & Eckols, S. L. (Eds.). (1997). Use typographic cueing devices to direct the user's attention. *Handbook of usability principles.* San Diego State University Foundation & California State Employment Development Department. <http://clipt.sdsu.edu/posit/tx/posit.qry?function=Detail&Layout1_uid1=38>.

Azevedo, R., & Bernard, R. M. (1995). A meta-analysis of the effects of feedback in computer-based instruction. *Journal of Educational Computing Research, 13*(2), 111–127.

Bloom, B. S., Mesia, B. B., & Krathwohl, D. R. (1964). *Taxonomy of educational objectives* [The Affective Domain & The Cognitive Domain (Two vols.)]. New York: David McKay.

Boden, A., Archwamety, T., & McFarland, M. (2000). Programmed instruction in secondary education: A meta-analysis of the impact of class size on its effectiveness. *Paper presented at the Annual Meeting of the National Association of School Psychologists, March 2000.* New Orleans.

Borg, W., & Gall, M. (1989). *Educational Research* (5th ed.). White Plains, New York: Longman Inc.

Bostow, D. E., Kritch, K. M., & Tompkins, B. F. (1995). Computers and pedagogy: Replacing telling with interactive computer-programmed instruction. *Behavior Research Methods, Instruments, & Computers, 27*(2), 297–300.

Burton, J. K., Moore, D. M., & Magliaro, S. G. (1996). Behaviorism and instructional technology. In D. Jonassen (Ed.), *Handbook of Research for Educational Communications and Technology* (Chapter 2). New York: Simon & Schuster Macmillan.

Butson, R. (2003). Learning objects: Weapons of mass instruction. *British Journal of Educational Technology, 34*(5), 667–669.

Cashen, V. M., & Leicht, K. L. (1970). Role of the isolation effect in a formal educational setting. *Journal of Educational Psychology, 61*(6), 484–486.

Chang, S. L., & Ley, K. (2006). A learning strategy to compensate for cognitive overload in online learning: Learner use of printed online materials. *Journal of Interactive Online Learning 5*(1), Retrieved August 2, 2006, http://www.ncolr.org/jiol/issues/PDF/5.1.8.pdf

Cho, Y. (1995). Learner control, cognitive processes, and hypertext learning environments. In *Emerging Technologies, Lifelong Learning, NECC '95.*

Paper presented at the Annual National Educational Computing Conference, June 1995. Baltimore.

Clark, R. (1983). Reconsidering research on learning from media. *Review of Educational Research, 53*(4), 445–459.

Cooper, J., Heron, T., & Heward, W. (1987). *Applied behavior analysis.* Columbus, Ohio: Merril.

Cronbach, L., & Snow, R. (1977). *Aptitudes and instructional methods: A handbook for research on interactions.* New York: Wiley & Sons.

Devilly, G. J. (2004). *The effect size generator for Windows: Version 2.3 (computer program)*. Australia: Centre for Neuropsychology, Swinburne University. <http://www.swin.edu.au/victims/resources/software/effectsize/effect_size_generator.html>.

Dewey, J. (1897). My pedagogic creed. *The School Journal, 54*(3), 77–80. <http://www.infed.org/archives/e-texts/e-dew-pc.htm>.

————. (1916). *Democracy and education.* New York: Macmillan. <http://www.ilt.columbia.edu/publications/dewey.html>.

Duffy, T. M., & Cunningham, D. J. (1996). Constructivism: Implications for the design and delivery of instruction. In D. H. Jonassen (Ed.), *Handbook of research for educational communications and technology* (Chapter 7). New York: Simon & Schuster Macmillan.

Durso, F. T., & Mellgren, R. L. (1989). *Thinking about research.* St. Paul, Minnesota: West Publishing.

Dyson, M. C., & Gregory, J. (2002). Typographic cueing on screen. *Visible Language, 36*(3), 326.

Ehrmann, S. C. (1995). Asking the right question: What does research tell us about technology and higher learning. *Change, The Magazine of Higher Learning, 27*(2), 20–27.

Fisher, S. G. (2000). Web-based training: One size does not fit all. In K. Mantyla (Ed.), *The 2000/2001 distance learning yearbook.* New York: McGraw-Hill.

Fowler, R., & Barker, A. (1974). Effectiveness of highlighting for retention of text material. *Journal of Applied Psychology, 59*(3), 358–364.

Gagné, R. (1985). *The conditions of learning* (4th ed.). New York: Holt, Rinehart & Winston.

Glynn, S. M., Britton, B. K., & Tillman, M. H. (1985). Typographic cues in text: Management of the reader's attention. In D. H. Jonassen (Ed.), The technology of text: Principles for structuring, designing, and displaying text (Vol. 2). Englewood Cliffs, New Jersey: Educational Technology Publications.

Goldberg, A. K. (2005). Exploring instructional design issues with Web-enhanced courses: What do faculty need in order to present materials on-line and what should they consider when doing so? *Journal of Interactive Online Learning* 4(1). <http://www.ncolr.org/jiol/issues/PDF/4.1.3.pdf> Retrieved April 4, 2006.

Gropper, G. L. (1987). A lesson based on a behavioral approach to instructional design. In C. M. Reigeluth (Ed.), *Instructional theories in action: Lessons illustrating selected theories and models* (Chapter 3). Hillsdale, New Jersey: Lawrence Erlbaum Associates.

Hartley, J. (1987). Designing electronic text: The role of print-based research. *Educational Communications and Technology Journal, 35*(1), 3–17.

Holland, J. G. (1967). A quantitative measure for programmed instruction. *American Educational Research Journal, 4*, 87–101.

Huitt, W., & Hummel, J. (1997). *An introduction to operant (instrumental) conditioning: Educational psychology interactive*. Valdosta, Georgia: Valdosta State University. <http://chiron.valdosta.edu/whuitt/col/behsys/operant.html>.

―――. (1998). *An overview of the behavioral perspective: Educational psychology interactive*. Valdosta, Georgia: Valdosta State University. <http://chiron.valdosta.edu/whuitt/col/behsys/behsys.html>.

Johnston, J. M., & Pennypacker, H. S. (1980). *Strategies and tactics of behavioral research*. New Jersey: Lawrence Erlbaum Associates, Inc.

Keller, F. S. (1968). Goodbye, Teacher… *Journal of Applied Behavioral Analysis, 1*(1), 79–89.

Kerlinger, F. N. (1986). *Foundations of behavioral research* (3rd ed.). New York: Holt, Rinehart & Winston.

Kozma, R. (1991). Learning with media. *Review of Educational Research, 61*(2), 179–211.

Kritch, K. M., & Bostow, D. E. (1994). *Creating computer programmed instruction* [Computer program]. Tampa, Florida: Customs Systems International, Inc.

―――. (1998). Degree of constructed-response interaction in computer-based programmed instruction. *Journal of Applied Behavior Analysis, 31*(3), 387–398.

Kritch, K. M., Bostow, D. E., & Dedrick, R. F. (1995). Level of interactivity of videodisc instruction on college students' recall of AIDS information. *Journal of Applied Behavior Analysis, 28*(1), 85–86.

Lunts, E. (2002). What does the literature say about the effectiveness of learner control in computer assisted instruction? *Electronic Journal for the Integration of Technology in Education, 1*(2), 59–75.

Lutz, J., Briggs, A., & Cain, K. (2003). An examination of the value of the generation effect for learning new material. *Journal of General Psychology, 130*(2), 171–188.

Manitoba Education, Citizenship and Youth (2001). Literacy learning through the six language arts. <http://www.edu.gov.mb.ca/ks4/cur/ela/docs/litlearn3.html>.

Mergel, B. (1998). Instructional design and learning theory. *Occasional paper, educational communications and technology.* University of Saskatchewan. <www.usask.ca/education/coursework/802papers/mergel/brenda.htm>.

Merrill, M. D. (1987). A lesson based on the component display theory. In C. M. Reigeluth (Ed.), *Instructional theories in action: Lessons illustrating selected theories and models* (Chapter 7). Hillsdale, New Jersey: Lawrence Erlbaum Associates.

Molenda, M. (2002). *A new framework for teaching in the cognitive domain.* Syracuse, New York: ERIC Clearing-house on Information & Technology, ERIC Document: ED 470 983.

Morey, E. H. (1996). Feedback Research. In D. H. Jonassen (Ed.), *Handbook of research for educational communications and technology* (Chapter 32). New York: Simon & Schuster Macmillan.

Parker, K. (2000). *Art, science and the importance of aesthetics in instructional design.* Occasional Paper, Graduate Student, University of South Florida.

Petry, B., Mouton, H., & Reigeluth, C. M. (1987). A Lesson Based on the Gagné-Briggs Theory of Instruction. In C. M. Reigeluth (Ed.), Instructional theories in action: Lessons illustrating selected theories and models (Chapter 2). Hillsdale, New Jersey: Lawrence Erlbaum Associates.

Rabinowitz, J. C., & Craik, F. I. M. (1986). Specific enhancement effects associated with word generation. *Journal of Memory and Language, 25*, 226–237.

Reeves, T. C. (1993). Psuedoscience in instructional technology: The case of learner control research. *In Proceedings of selected research and development presentations at the 1993 convention of the Association for Educational Communications and Technology, January 1993*, New Orleans.

Rickards, J. P., & August, J. G. (1975). Generative underlining strategies in prose recall. *Journal of Educational Psychology, 67*(8), 860–865.

Saba, F. (2000). Research in distance education: A status report. *International Review of Research in Open and Distance Learning, 1*(1). <http://www.irrodl.org/content/v1.1/farhad.html>.

Siemens, G. (2003). Evaluating media characteristics: Using multimedia to achieve learning outcomes. *Paper presented at AMTEC 2002.* <http://www.elearnspace.org/Articles/mediacharacteristics.htm>.

Shoffner, M. B., Jones, M., & Harmon, S. W. (2000). Implications of new and emerging technologies for learning and cognition. *Journal of Electronic Publishing, 6*(1). <http://www.press.umich.edu/jep/06-01/shoffner.html>.

Skinner, B. F. (1938). *The behavior of organisms.* New York: Appleton.

———. (1950). Are theories of learning necessary? *Psychological Review, 57*(4), 193–216. <http://psychclassics.yorku.ca/Skinner/Theories/>.

———. (1968). *The technology of teaching.* New York: Meredith.

———. (1969). *Contingencies of reinforcement: A theoretical analysis* [The Century Psychology Series]. New York: Appleton.

———. (1972). *Cumulative Record* [The Century Psychology Series]. New York: Appleton.

Slavin, R. E. (2000). *Educational psychology: Theory and Practice* (6th ed.). Needham Heights, Massachusetts: Allyn & Bacon.

Sulzer-Azaroff, B., & Mayer, R. (1991). *Behavior analysis for lasting change.* Chicago: Holt, Rinehart and Winston.

Thomas, D. L., & Bostow, D. E. (1991). Evaluation of pre-therapy computer-interactive instruction. *Journal of Computer-Based Instruction, 18*(2), 66–70.

Thompson, A., Simonson, M., & Hargrave, C. (1996). *Educational technology: A review of the research* (2nd ed.). Washington, D.C.: Association for Educational Communications and Technology.

Tudor, R. M. (1995). Isolating the effects of active responding in computer-based instruction. *Journal of Applied Behavior Analysis, 28*(3), 343–344.

Tudor, R. M., & Bostow, D. E. (1991). Computer-programmed instruction: The relation of required interaction to practical application. *Journal of Applied Behavior Analysis, 24*(2), 361–368.

Wegner, S. B., & Holloway, K. C. (1999). The effects of internet-based instruction on student learning. *Journal of Asynchronous Learning Networks, 3*(2), 98–106. <http://www.sloan-c.org/publications/jaln/v3n2/pdf/v3n2_wegner.pdf>.

Williams, M. D. (1996). Learner-control and instructional technologies. In
    D. H. Jonassen (Ed.), *Handbook of Research for Educational Communications
    and Technology* (Chapter 33). New York: Simon & Schuster Macmillan.

Wisher, R. A., & Champagne, M. (2000). Distance learning and training: An
    evaluation perspective. In S. Tobias, & J. Fletcher, (Eds.), *Training and
    retraining: A handbook for business, industry, government, and military.*
    New York: Macmillan.

INDEX

Printed in the United States
85198LV00009B